ASSASSINATION OF THE
PRIME MINISTER

Assassination of the Prime Minister

The Shocking Death of Spencer Perceval

MOLLIE GILLEN

SIDGWICK & JACKSON

LONDON

First published in Great Britain in 1972

Copyright © 1972 Mollie Gillen

ISBN 0 283 97881 3

Printed in Great Britain by
William Clowes & Sons, Limited, London, Beccles and Colchester
for Sidgwick and Jackson Limited
1 Tavistock Chambers, Bloomsbury Way
London WC1A 2SG

To Gerard Young,
author, historian and friend,
whose death leaves an unfillable gap.

I am one, my liege,
Whom the vile blows and buffets of the world
Have so incens'd that I am reckless what
I do to spite the world.

The Second Murderer, *Macbeth*, III, i

Acknowledgements

RECOGNITION of the courtesy and willing assistance of a host of people too numerous to identify fully must fall far short of my indebtedness to them; but I must record particular thanks to James Howgego, Assistant Librarian in charge of maps and prints at the Guildhall Library, and his assistant, Ralph Hyde; to Mrs Winnifred Stevens, whose familiarity with archives in Liverpool and district was placed so generously at my service; to Mrs Eve Jennings, Assistant Archivist at the Greater London Record Office (Middlesex Records); to P. J. Locke, County Archivist at Huntingdon, and his assistant Mrs Cottrell; to D. J. Bryant, Chief Librarian, Kingston upon Hull City Libraries, and D.C.L. Holland, Librarian of the House of Commons; to the Reverend S. A. Griffiths, vicar of the Church of St Mary the Virgin at St Neots, who opened to me the church and the parish registers, to Dr Ida Macalpine and Dr Richard Hunter for their interest and assistance; to Dr Barry Hollingsworth, Department of Russian Studies, University of Manchester, and Professor K. A. Papmehl, Department of Russian Studies, University of Western Ontario, who pointed me to new sources of information; to the Directors of Butterworth and Co. (Publishers) Ltd, for making available their company archives; to the staffs of the Metropolitan Toronto Library, the University of Toronto Library, the British Museum, the Public Record Office, the India Office Records, the Marylebone Public Library, the Liverpool City Library; to all the librarians and county archivists across England and in Ireland who responded so promptly with information: to

publishers and editors of the contemporary correspondence and
memoirs from which I learned so much. I am also indebted to
Doris Anderson, editor of *Chatelaine*, for generously granting me
the leave of absence necessary to complete this work.

Acknowledgements are due to the Metropolitan Toronto Library
Board for plates 5a and 5b, 6b and d, 7, 10, 11a, 12, 14, 15, 16a and b;
to the National Portrait Gallery for plate 1; to the Guildhall Library
for plate 2; to Dr Ida Macalpine for plates 3a and 8a, from pamphlets in her possession; to Sir John Heygate for plate 6a; to the British
Museum for plates 3b, 4, 8b and 13; to the City of Norwich Museums
for plate 6e; to the *Illustrated London News* for plate 7; to the
Greater London Council for plates 9; to Chas. J. Sawyer, No. 1,
Grafton St, London W.1 for plate 11b; to the Public Record Office
for plate 16a.

Contents

List of Illustrations

Preface

It is not my intention in this study to try to 'rehabilitate' John Bellingham, the assassin of Spencer Perceval, nor even to claim that *tout comprendre* is necessarily *tout pardonner*. It is to try to understand him, and in some measure to try to recapture the shock and panic that swept across Britain in much the same way and for much the same reason as the horror throughout the whole world after the assassination of John Fitzgerald Kennedy. There was the same sense of utter disbelief, the same fear that the lone gunman was not alone, but spearheaded a larger, organized attack: the same grief, the same foreboding uncertainty about the future, the fear that this was the iceberg tip of a tremendous and imminent threat to the very existence of orderly life in the nation.

The words of those who wrote in the aftermath of tragedy, whether journalist, diarist, or someone writing a private letter, still ring with the anguish, the anger, the apprehension of those whose shaking hands committed them to paper. Few readers to-day can have the privilege of reading them in the original from the age-softened pages of contemporary journals, in the fading ink of personal letters. Where possible, I have let them tell their own story in their own words. As one of the *Times Literary Supplement*'s anonymous reviewers recently remarked, 'Anyone who has cause to consult the newspaper files of the early nineteenth century is likely to admire the freshness and vigour of the writing as well as the indestructibility of the newsprint.' There is no better way to relive a moment in history than to listen to the words of those who lived when it was happening.

'If people really want to understand the world they live in,' wrote another perceptive T.L.S. reviewer, 'they will need to read history.' Those who wring hands over the sickness of today's society might be a little more satisfied of progress, perhaps, were they aware of past horrors to be found in penal laws, social conditions, and the ever-present threat and tragedy of diseases incurable then and conquered now. We have not achieved Utopia, but we have moved forward.

Author's Note

In quoting from printed material, I have followed exactly the spelling and punctuation given. Where manuscript sources are quoted, I have updated punctuation, but not spelling. All quotations, except comments from later legal critics, are from contemporary sources, and none of the dialogue is 'fictionalized'.

CHAPTER ONE

A most atrocious and afflicting event

WITNESSES recalled later – trying to put together into some kind of sequence the shattering events of the evening of 11 May 1812 – that the lobby of the House of Commons had been unusually empty; not more than twenty or thirty people were passing through or waiting there for various reasons [1]*. Attendance in the House itself, too, was thin. Only about 60 of the 658 Members of Parliament were present for the continuation of the inquiry into the controversial Orders in Council (brought in by the Whigs in 1807 but continued and expanded by the Tory government later that year) which were attempting to counter retaliatory Napoleonic decrees by increased blockade and severe impositions on neutral shipping.

A motion in March by Henry Brougham – Member for Camelford and relentless opponent of Government policy – for a select committee 'to inquire into the present state of the commerce and manufactures of the country with reference to the effects of the Orders in Council' had resulted instead in a committee of the whole House, which had begun its sittings on the previous Tuesday. At the beginning of this Monday session, the House had

* These figures refer to the Notes section on pp. 166–171.

resolved itself into committee under the chairmanship of Mr Thomas Babington, Member for Leicester. Mr Brougham had finished his examination of the first witness, Robert Hamilton, a potter from Stoke-on-Trent in Staffordshire, on his petition for repeal of the Orders (which, he claimed, were ruining trade and creating dreadful hardships across the country), and Mr James Stephen (Grinstead) had just launched into cross-examination, when a sound like a pistol shot was heard from somewhere outside.

An unusual rushing and confusion immediately followed from the direction of the lobby, and alarmed voices – 'a perfect Babel' – were heard calling. Heads turned uncertainly towards the door, and the Members exchanged startled, inquiring glances. A few leaped up and ran out of the Chamber. The rest, though with wandering attention, tried to continue the business of the day, unable to believe that the disturbance could be a serious one. Then a whisper ran round the Chamber – someone had been shot. Despite cries of 'Order, Order', a rush started between the Bar of the House and the door into the lobby. People came clattering down the stairs from the gallery, and the examination came to an abrupt halt.

In the House of Lords on the other side of the lobby, several passages away, where the Peers were also discussing the Orders in Council, a stunned silence followed the sound of the shot. No one was, in fact, quite certain that it had been a shot; but that something untoward was taking place was evident from the bustle and babble of voices now growing in volume. A voice outside the Chamber was then heard, crying, 'Mr Perceval is shot – Mr Perceval is shot!' Next moment, an officer of the House of Commons burst through the door in the most extreme agitation. Almost all the Peers had already risen in dismay from their seats. They now crowded around the newcomer, trying to get a coherent account of what had happened.

He had been standing in the lobby, the gentleman said in a distraught voice, when someone had fired a pistol at the Prime Minister, who then staggered a few paces, cried out something that sounded like 'Murder!' and fell on his face on the floor.

Several of the Peers had hurried out at the first sound of trouble. Most of the rest now followed in a rush, leaving only Lord Chancellor Eldon and three bishops continuing their anxious inquiries at the Bar of the House. Though it might prove to be true that, incredibly, Perceval had been shot, there was still hope that he might have been wounded only. But as those who had left the House began slowly returning, with pale, shocked faces, it was apparent from their expressions that no hope remained.

It had been about a quarter past five when Perceval – Spencer Perceval, First Lord of the Treasury, Chancellor of the Exchequer and Prime Minister of Great Britain – had briskly mounted the short flight of stone steps into the lobby leading to the House of Commons. Henry Brougham, annoyed by the absence of Mr Perceval who, he said later, had failed for the second time to be present at the time of four-thirty agreed upon to begin debate on the Orders in Council, had notified the Secretary of the Treasury that he would go on regardless. The messenger sent by the Secretary to remind Perceval had seen the short, slight figure of the Prime Minister in Parliament Street, walking the short distance from his house in Downing Street. Told of Brougham's complaint, Perceval hurried his pace to lose as little time as possible.

Tall folding doors led into the lobby. The left-hand panel was fastened shut, the right-hand panel could be pushed open. Perceval handed his greatcoat to the officer stationed outside the door, and mounted the steps just behind William Jerdan, a journalist for the *British Press*. When Jerdan, pushing open the door, half turned and recognized the Prime Minister, he stood aside to allow Perceval to precede him, and received a bow and a pleasant smile.

To the right of the door a small knot of men had gathered, including Mr Boys, a solicitor from Margate, waiting to discuss a bill dealing with the pier and harbour at the seaside town. A Mayfair solicitor, Henry Burgess, stood near the door to the House, hoping to speak later to Samuel Whitbread. Across the lobby, Lord Francis Osborne and Mr Nicholas Colborne, having left the House, were proceeding towards the exit door; Colborne stopped for a moment near one of the four pillars that supported the ceiling in the centre of the lobby to speak to someone he knew. Just behind him, William Smith, Member for Norwich, had paused momentarily on his way into the Chamber to talk to a friend. He heard the report of a pistol, and turned to observe a cluster of people milling around near the door at the lobby entrance. Several voices cried out 'Shut the door – let no one escape!' and at that moment one man broke away from the group and came staggering towards Mr Smith, his head turning from one side to the other as if seeking refuge. He muttered something that sounded to Smith like 'Murder', and at once fell face downwards on the floor.

Smith, taken completely aback and expecting the man to get back to his feet, did nothing for an astounded moment. Then, motioning to a bystander (this was Francis Phillips of Longsight Hall, near Manchester, who had been standing near the fireplace on the left of the lobby and had rushed forward when he saw the victim fall), Smith, with Phillips, turned him face upwards and realized that the man they held was the Prime Minister.

Other horrified people (Nicholas Colborne, several of the officers of the House) now pressed forward to help. With Smith supporting him on the right and Phillips on the left, Perceval was carried into the office of the Speaker's secretary and placed in a sitting position on a table, his feet on two chairs, resting on the arms of his supporters who seated themselves on the table on either side of the stricken man. The Prime Minister's face

was, by this time, perfectly pale, the blood issuing in small quantities from each corner of his mouth [Mr Smith reported later] and . . . there was not, probably, more than two or three minutes elapsed from the firing of the pistol when there was scarcely any signs of life remaining. His eyes were still open, but he did not appear to know witness, nor to take any notice of any person about him, nor had he uttered the least articulate sound from the moment he fell. A few convulsive sobs which lasted, perhaps, three or four minutes, together with a scarcely perceptible pulse, were the only signs of life that appeared then, and those continued but a very short time longer; and when witness felt Mr Perceval's wrist for the last time, just before Mr Lynn, the surgeon, arrived, it appeared to him that he was totally dead [2].

William Lynn, the surgeon who lived at No. 15 in nearby Great George Street, had been summoned at once (indeed, a Mr Spottis-wood, 'a Gentleman of great respectability', who had observed the two tall men running through Westminster Hall in search of medical aid, had suspected that they might be villains escaping justice, and volunteered to identify them if necessary). But except for noting that Perceval's white waistcoat was bloody, that there was 'a wound on the skin, about over the left side, near the breast bone [that] had the appearance of a large pistol-ball having entered', and examining his pulse, Surgeon Lynn could do nothing but give his official medical verdict that Perceval was quite dead. A probe inserted into the wound revealed that the ball had passed obliquely downwards and inwards in the direction of the heart to a depth of three inches. 'I have no doubt', declared Mr Lynn later, 'that it caused his death.'

In the lobby and in both Houses, confusion and panic were mounting. Vincent George Dowling, a reporter for the *Day*, had pelted down from the gallery on hearing the shot. General Isaac Gascoyne, Member for Liverpool, writing a letter in the smoking room above the lobby, had started up, crying, 'That is a pistol; what can it mean?' and rushed downstairs. Joseph Hume (Weymouth), with other horrified Members, had hurried from the Chamber as soon as the alarm had been raised. John Norris, a frequent visitor to the strangers' gallery, and at the crucial moment twenty steps into the upper lobby leading to the gallery, stopped in his tracks when he heard the shot.

Jerdan, though immediately behind Perceval, would recall afterwards with disbelief that he had not heard any sound at all. He did, however, see a small curl of smoke, saw Perceval reel slightly back towards the left, heard him say faintly, 'O God!' or 'O my God!', saw him lurch forward and collapse at the feet of William Smith. Seeing that others had moved at once to assist the fallen man, Jerdan checked his impulsive rush to help. The lobby was swarming with appalled and whitefaced men, Members from the House, Peers from the Lords, strangers from the gallery, witnesses, reporters, officers, calling out, 'Who did it? Which is the man? Where is he? Who is he?' A gentleman at the far left-hand corner of the lobby (unknown to Jerdan at the time but later identified as Mr Eastaff, a clerk of the Vote Office) cried out, 'That is the man!' and pointed to a tall, thin person who was by now sitting on a bench against the wall beside the fireplace. Jerdan at once went over and seized him by the collar.

He had made no attempt to escape. 'If he had risen in a minute or two afterwards, and walked quietly out into the street, he would have escaped, and the committer of the murder would never have been known unless he had chosen to divulge it' [3].

The man appeared to be about five feet eight or nine inches in height, his age somewhere between thirty and forty. He was dressed 'like a decent mechanic' in a dark-coloured coat. His face was long and thin, with a sallow complexion, an aquiline nose, prominent dark blue eyes beneath overhanging brows, and his upper lip noticeably projected over the lower one. His dark hair was cut short.

Though he now sat quietly on the bench by the fireplace ('A Mouse might have secured him with a bit of Thread,' wrote Henry Burgess, scribbling a hasty letter to his friend and client Richard Brinsley Sheridan later that evening [4]) it was evident that he was under strong emotion. 'Large drops of agonizing sweat ran down his pallid face,' Jerdan saw.

> ... The former resembled rain-drops on a window, in a heavy storm ... the latter was of the cadaverous hue of the tomb; and, from the bottom of his chest to his gorge, rose and fell a spasmodic action, as if a body as large as the hand were choking him with every breath. The miserable creature struck his chest repeatedly with his palm, as if to abate this sensation. Never, on earth, I believe, was seen a more terrible example of over-wrought suffering: yet, in language he was perfectly cool and collected [5].

He was by now surrounded by a dozen stricken and angry men, his coat and shirt roughly pulled open so that he was bared to the breast. Henry Burgess removed the pistol, still warm, from where it lay on the bench beneath his hand. Dowling, who had seized him on the other side from Jerdan, took from him 'a plain but powerful opera glass in a red case', handed it to Jerdan, and, with Burgess, began to search his clothes. Gascoyne, excited and belligerent, seized him so violently when Dowling released his hold to make the search of his person that he almost broke the man's arm. 'You need not press me,' the prisoner said. 'I submit myself to justice.'

Someone now came from the Speaker's room with the doctor's tragic verdict. 'Mr Perceval is dead! Villain, how could you destroy so good a man, and make a family of ten or twelve children orphans?' The prisoner replied mournfully, 'I am sorry for it,' and in words that were remembered variously and in varying sequences by the different hearers afterwards, he added, 'I am the unfortunate man – I wish I were in Mr Perceval's place. My name is John Bellingham; it is a private injury – I know what I have done. It was a denial of justice on the part of Government.'

Search of his pockets yielded an assortment of objects: a guinea in gold, a one-pound note, one bank token for 5s. 6d. and two for 1s. 6d., a small penknife, a bunch of keys, a pencil. In the pocket of his small-clothes, Dowling found a second pistol, pair to the fatal weapon and fully loaded. Gascoyne discovered a bundle of papers tied with red tape, and these, removed with some difficulty because the prisoner held them high over his head in an effort to retain them against the manhandling he was receiving from all sides, were handed to Joseph Hume. Hume enclosed them in a sheet of paper closed with his own seal and delivered them in turn to the Foreign Secretary, Lord Castlereagh.

By this time the House of Commons was in a state of near-pandemonium. No one knew whether the assassination was an isolated crime or the first sign of a vast plot that was about to erupt and bring down a red-hot flow of insurrection on the whole country. Reaction against the Orders in Council – those counter-moves to Napoleonic blockade decrees – had been rumbling with louder and louder noise and fury. Could it be possible that this assassin was the spearhead of organized attack?

Almost all the journals for months past had been working up to a crescendo of concern – apprehensive, apologetic, apoplectic or vitriolic according to their political views – over the unsatisfactory progress of the war with France, the low state of the national economy, and the rising and increasingly alarming unrest among the lower orders. Many of these had already shown themselves irresponsibly unwilling to accept continued poverty and starvation in decent silence, and had resorted to violent action in various parts of the kingdom. In Nottingham, for instance, framebreakers had made honest folk afraid to go to bed at night, and indeed were becoming damnably cunning, attacking in the absence of owners and fleeing before anyone, even the troops sent to deal with the marauders, could catch them. With a precision impudently assumed from their military betters, armed parties in the Huddersfield area were breaking into mills on errands of destruction, numbering smartly from the left and marching off in good order before any action could be taken to stop them. Outraged letters from local authorities had begun to clutter up Home Office files.

A recalcitrant America, too, was causing serious concern on the international front. The smouldering friction from continuing violations of the Treaty of Paris by both sides since 1783 was ready to flame into war, ignited by the final spark of British insistence on boarding neutral vessels in a search for contraband and deserters. No wonder, after the Prime Minister had been murdered just outside the door of the Chamber, panic ensued. 'Doors were guarded, messengers were running to and fro – all was disorder.'

Though Members as yet had no clear idea of how to handle this unprecedented situation, an insistent clamour now arose that the prisoner should be brought to the Bar of the House. Someone had had the forethought to put the question so that the committee chairman could properly leave the chair; the motion being instantly carried, the Speaker, Charles Abbot, who had retired when the House went into committee, now returned to the Chamber and resumed his seat.

In the confusion, Richard Taylor, the elderly doorkeeper, was for once unable to collect his wits, and allowed all comers into the House. Amid continuous tumult and a swelling crowd of strangers (even a few of the Peers) who in some cases were actually mingling with the Members in the body of the House, Bellingham was brought in, preceded by Francis John Colman, the Serjeant-at-Arms, escorted by the messengers Wright and Skelton, and still firmly clutched by Jerdan; possibly also by Gascoyne – his report of the part he played in the event was in some particulars gently queried by Jerdan when he wrote his version at a later date, noting that 'the consternation that prevailed might well excuse imperfection of memory, and the blending of after hearsay with what was actually seen and done' [6].

Some semblance of order at last having been restored, and most of the Members having taken their seats, Gascoyne (who seems not to have heard Bellingham's statement of his name in the lobby) now walked up to the dishevelled prisoner, saying, 'I think I know the villain. Is not your name Bellingham?' The latter, by this time entirely composed, merely nodded, resting his hands on the Bar and looking steadily towards the Speaker.

It was then decided that the rules of the House would not allow examination of the prisoner, who was not in formal legal custody.

When silence had been restored, the Speaker ordered that he be taken to the prison room of the Serjeant-at-Arms beyond the upper lobby, where witnesses could be examined by any of the Members who were Middlesex magistrates. He also suggested that the route to the prison room should be by such passages as would avoid the crowded lobby and the possibility of rescue by accomplices, and that the escort group should be preceded by Members to make sure the passages were clear. A rush of volunteers to carry out this order was stopped by Samuel Whitbread's sensible suggestion that the preceding and following parties be specifically named; between these two groups, escorted by the Serjeant-at-Arms and several messengers, Bellingham was removed from the Chamber, and the House adjourned.

In the House of Lords, too, procedure had disintegrated in grief and uncertainty, and small groups of Noble Lords stood around in agitated private conversation as others came and went. 'The consternation was great; the appearance of most present ghastly. I remember', recalled Lord Holland, 'I wondered to myself whether my face was as much altered as those of the persons around me' [7]. At length the Lord Chancellor quitted the Woolsack, and 'under strong impressions of grief and agitation', apologized for any trespass upon their lordships' orders he might be committing in requesting that 'the doors of the House, and of the avenues immediately leading to it' be closed 'with a view, as far as possible, to the prevention of the immediate commission of further mischief'.

In such an unprecedented situation, debate was confused about what to do next. Before adjournment, which seemed the logical next step, their lordships thought it would be proper to address the Prince Regent with 'the sentiments of the House on the melancholy and horrid occurrence'. For this to be done, it was necessary to have the horrid occurrence formally established.

The Duke of Cumberland therefore rose to state, with strong emotion, that he had just seen 'my Right Honourable Friend Mr Perceval wounded and dead!' This was not, however, considered sufficient evidence of the manner in which the Prime Minister had met that death. Lord Ellenborough, Lord Chief Justice and Speaker of the House, who had come hurriedly into the Chamber from a sitting in his Court of King's Bench, 'expressed his decided opinion that an examination at the Bar, as to the fact, would be the most proper and regular course'.

Accordingly, Richard Taylor, senior doorkeeper of the House of Commons, who had witnessed the tragedy, was summoned. Mr Taylor stated that he had seen the pistol, seen and heard it go off, and seen Perceval fall immediately afterwards. The point having been formally established, and an humble address to the Prince Regent (who was at Carlton House and not, as some writers have believed, quaking in Brighton), expressing regret and abhorrence having been moved by the Earl of Radnor and carried unanimously, this House, too, adjourned until the morrow.

CHAPTER TWO

I am a most unfortunate man

THE prison room where the examination now took place soon became so crowded with witnesses and spectators that the doors were locked, leaving outside a press of curious and disappointed people. Those who got in found the proceedings a painful ordeal, tears and distress on every face, tremors in every voice. William Jerdan, in the aftermath of shock, leaned against a baluster and was very near to fainting until an observant friend, Mr (later Sir Charles) Burrell, Member for New Shoreham, brought him a glass of water.

Several magistrates took part in the examination. Mr Alderman Combe (Harvey Christian Combe, one of the City of London Members of Parliament) took the chair, assisted by the diminutive fifty-five-year-old Michael Angelo Taylor, Member for Ilchester, and the Serjeant-at-Arms of the House of Lords, William Watson, who had been invited to attend. While messengers were dispatched to Bellingham's lodgings at No. 9, New Millman Street, Bedford Row, 'to secure whatever papers or property might there be found', and to Bow Street for police officers and a pair of handcuffs, the principal witnesses gave their evidence. Michael Sexton, a journeyman bookseller of No. 12, China Row, Lambeth, and Francis Romilly, clerk to a gentleman residing at No. 56, Gower Street, who had been in the lobby and seen two flashes as the pistol fired, were also among those examined.

Bellingham, warned by Sir John Coxe Hippisley, the Member

for Sudbury, 'not to say anything to criminate himself', tranquilly agreed with or commented on the evidence; he qualified the statement made by Burgess ('Perhaps Mr Burgess was less agitated than I was, but I think he took the pistol from my hand, and not from the bench under me'); and corroborated the strength of Gascoyne's grasp ('He held him with so much violence, that he was apprehensive his arm would be broken'). Gascoyne recalled that 'he had seen Bellingham often, and that he had received many petitions and memorials from him respecting some claims upon government, which he ought to be allowed. These demands . . . originated in services alleged to be performed by the criminal in Russia, for which he complains that he has obtained no remuneration.'

His calm impressed everyone. 'Not the slightest symptom of remorse appeared in the wretch, notwithstanding the universal horror which his atrocity had produced on all that surrounded him.' Only when Francis Phillips made his statement, 'I supported Mr Perceval into the secretary's room, and in a few moments he died in my arms,' did Bellingham show any emotion. At these words, he shed some tears.

Joseph Hume produced the papers taken from the prisoner. Charles Burrell handed over the pistol that had fired the fatal shot, Dowling the pistol found in the pocket of his breeches. John Vickery, the Bow Street officer who had searched Bellingham's room at his lodgings, now arrived with what he had found, tied up in a handkerchief. This bundle was handed to Lord Castlereagh for submission to the Privy Council, its contents to be eventually produced at Bellingham's trial.

The prisoner, though warned again by Sir John Hippisley not to say anything that might injure his case, launched into the beginning of a full defence of his action.

I have admitted the fact – I admit the fact, but wish, with permission, to state something in my justification. I have been denied the redress of my grievances by Government; I have been ill-treated. They all know who I am, and what I am, through the Secretary of State and Mr Becket, with whom I have had frequent communications. They knew of this fact six weeks ago, through the Magistrates of Bow Street. I was accused most wrongfully by a Governor-General in Russia in a letter from Archangel to Riga [*sic*], and have sought redress in vain. I am a most unfortunate man and feel here (placing his hand on his breast) sufficient justification for what I have done.

He explained earnestly, as if expecting reasonable men to understand his predicament, that for the past two years he had been applying to every source possible for compensation for his sufferings. When he had exhausted all routine approaches, realized at last that no aid could be expected, and was told that he might do his worst, he took the statement literally. 'The Police Officers and Secretary of State might have known what would happen a fortnight past.' He added, as if it were a reasonable corollary, 'I have obeyed them. I have done my worst, and I rejoice in the deed.'

At this point, Lord Castlereagh interrupted to explain that what was wanted just now was not a defence but a contradiction of the accusation of murder if he could make one. Bellingham therefore ended by saying simply, 'Since it seems best to you that I should not now explain the causes of my conduct, I will leave it until the day of my trial, when my country will have an opportunity of judging whether I am right or wrong' [8].

He was now permitted to dress, and the Bow Street officers, Vickery, and one of the two Adkins brothers, William or Harry, having been called in, he was handcuffed. He asked that his money should be returned to him but Burgess, who had it, had already left, and Whitbread promised it would be returned to him in the morning. Whitbread also assured him that Mr Combe would see that he was properly represented by counsel.

His remarkable composure continued. When he heard that John Vickery had questioned a woman about his private affairs (possibly his landlady, more probably Mary Stevens, a Liverpool friend in London at that time on business), he complained vigorously. He appeared mollified, however, when he heard that the woman's statements referred merely to a memorandum of twenty pounds due to him by a Mr Wilson, about which he said he knew, and which she was holding for him. Except on the subject of the assassination and his reasons for it, he was remarkably lucid and clear-headed. Some observers took this as evidence of sanity: others the very opposite, maintaining that no sane man could preserve such unruffled calm after such a deed.

Much frantic flurry had been going on elsewhere in the meantime, and messengers sent flying in all directions. One went to Richmond to summon Viscount Sidmouth, Lord President of Council, another to delay departure of the mail coaches until dispatches could be prepared with instructions to civil and military authorities everywhere. Various noble gentlemen – the Earls of Derby and Stamford, and Earl Fitzwilliam – departed hurriedly for their respective counties 'to exert their authority as Lords Lieutenants, to restore tranquillity'. The gates of St James's Park were closed by eight o'clock, and the Foot Guards, the City Militia, and several bodies of volunteers, including the Duke of Sussex's Royal North Britons, were called out 'to preserve the peace of the Metropolis'. Another messenger hurried to order out the Horse Guards; by six o'clock the alarm had spread to the streets, and a continually enlarging crowd thronging the environs of Westminster was threatening to turn into an undisciplined and possibly dangerous mob.

Though some were in tears, the crowd was in general becoming hostile and hard to control, filling all the nearby streets and milling about the Parliament Buildings with such pressure that the doors of Westminster Hall were locked, and constables placed at all entrances. When the hackney coach ordered by the magistrates to take Bellingham to the Prison of Newgate in the City appeared shortly after eight o'clock at the iron gates in lower Palace Yard, and an officer got in, some of the mob promptly climbed up and tried to open the door on the opposite side to rescue the prisoner they thought was within.

> By main force, only, could they be prevented from mounting the coach-box, clinging to the wheels, and even entering the coach to shake hands with and congratulate the murderer on his deed. They were whipped off; beaten off – there was no other course left – amid the execrations of the mob on the police and the vociferated applause and hurrahs for Bellingham *and Burdett*: for it is a remarkable circumstance, that this man bears so strong a general resemblance to the demagogue Baronet that – as I was told by one who knows Sir Francis and has seen Bellingham – he might, at first sight, be taken for him [9].

The likeness was remarked on by more than one observer.

Other plans had to be made. 'The crowd, which was at first composed of decent people, had been gradually swelled by a concourse of pick-pockets and the lower orders, who . . . were so exceedingly troublesome and even dangerous, that it was not deemed advisable to send [Bellingham] to Newgate in the manner intended.' The officers attending the coach prudently withdrew, and advised the magistrates to consider another method of conveyance. The empty coach was rapidly driven away.

A party of Life Guards had by now arrived, and, by forming a semi-circle in lower Palace Yard, they had managed to move the crowd back. 'Among the multitude, however, whom the news of so strange and sudden a catastrophe had soon collected in the street, and about the avenues of the House, the most savage expressions of joy and exultation were heard; accompanied with regret that others, and particularly the Attorney-General [Sir Vicary Gibbs], had not shared the same fate,' commented the law reformer and Member of Parliament, Samuel Romilly, next day [10]. The cries of 'Burdett for ever!' were well calculated to worry the Government; the radical Whig baronet's name had already been the rallying cry for recent serious riots. The reaction of the populace, in fact, was adding to the fears and tremors rippling through both Houses of Parliament. Although the first examination of the assassin had brought a swift glimmer of relief from the threat of a vast conspiracy behind his act, nothing was yet certain. And if an uprising was not actually a planned one, the rising babble from the streets could yet prove to be the beginnings of riot sparked spontaneously by the assassin's act. People could be heard shouting for Bellingham as if he had performed some deed of heroism. One man was arrested, charged with having cried out, 'Oh! I will fire my gun to-morrow: I did not think there was an Englishman left that had such a heart. He' (alluding to the murderer of Mr Perceval) 'could not have shot a greater rascal!'

Lord Clive, who had cancelled a dinner engagement to rush to the House, now offered the use of his 'chariot' to take the assassin away from Westminster [11]. Accordingly, Bellingham was taken out around midnight through the Speaker's Court and sent on his way accompanied in the coach by Michael Angelo Taylor, who had committed him, Stephen Lavender, the Chief Constable of Police, a King's Messenger named Ross, and Lord Clive. Two policemen stood behind the carriage, one sat on the box, and the cavalcade set off surrounded by a strong escort of Dragoon Guards under the command of Colonel Barton.

The rumour of assassination started a rush of visiting all over London – 'one might have supposed there were electric telegraphs' [12] – distraught people calling on friends by carriage or on foot to inquire about or to impart the dreadful news. On return home from a visit to his niece and nephew, the artist Joseph Farington found that some friends had called earlier to leave a paper with particulars of the assassination, and spent the rest of the evening discussing nothing else [13]. In another part of London, Lady Jerningham rushed to her pen. 'Henry Came flying into the Parlour yesterday before six o'clock with this horrible intelligence, and, as He was not in the House, I was in hopes it Could not be true. But an hour after the evening Papers were Cried about the Streets with this horrid addition' [14].

Queen Charlotte, receiving the information at half past ten from the Duke of Cambridge, who, dispatched by the Prince Regent, had sped out to Windsor in a chaise and four, 'was so much affected, that she withdrew to her private apartments, and did not join the company of her family at supper' [15]. In North Audley Street, Mary Berry had at first doubted the written message she had received from a friend while dining with her father and her sister Agnes, but knew something was amiss when her servant got the message from Mr Villiers's valet. After dinner she set out for the Villiers's home, and later went on to that of another friend. Both residences were full of people who had been in the House and were agog with I-was-there realism in telling the story. 'This deed, though horrible,' moralized Miss Berry in her journal that night, 'is unfortunately one of all countries, and is not without its parallel even here. But that which is not so, is the manner in which the populace took it, who surrounded the Houses of Parliament. They appear so very little shocked' [16].

The fear and uncertainty that settled with the gloom over London that night lay beneath the words that the Honourable Frances Calvert inscribed in her diary. 'Nobody knows at present whether it was the sole act of this man, or whether it is a plot. At all events, independent of the horrible thing it is, it is very alarming the guards were *all* out last night for fear of any tumult' [17].

When the news reached the City, the Lord Mayor, Claudius

Stephen Hunter, issued orders through the marshalmen and beadles to call all the constables into attendance at the watch-houses. Both sheriffs, William Heygate and Samuel Birch, went at once to the Mansion House for discussion, and then to Newgate to arrange for Bellingham's reception and for special precautions against any opportunity for suicide. This, it would transpire, was the furthest thing from Bellingham's mind, so assured was he of the justice of his action. To everyone who would listen he repeated with a fearful calm, with an almost condescending pity for every-one's inability to understand, the justice of the course he said he had been forced to take, and the certainty that he would be exon-erated at his trial.

Arrived at Newgate, where another crowd had gathered and where the Horse Guards now paraded for security, he was re-ceived by the keeper, John Addison Newman, and lodged in a strong room with a stone floor next to the chapel, double-ironed, and attended throughout the night by two of the keepers and the principal turnkey, on the orders of the Cabinet Council. He par-took of refreshments offered by Newman, and then went to bed, where he promptly fell asleep.

He was probably the calmest person in London.

CHAPTER THREE

Please to add the prayer book

AFTER it was certain that nothing could be done for the Prime Minister, now dead at not quite fifty, his body had been removed from the table in the Speaker's secretary's room to a 'sopha' in the Speaker's drawing-room, where his elder brother Lord Arden remained bending over it and weeping in anguish. The task of breaking the news to Jane Perceval had fallen to Lord Redesdale, whose wife Frances was a sister of Perceval. He had found Mrs Perceval just returned from a visit to her friend Frederica Ryder, wife of her husband's Home Secretary, Richard Ryder.

> Dear Walpole [wrote Lord Redesdale that night from the house on Downing Street to another of Perceval's brothers-in-law] The contents of this letter must give you the greatest distress, & it will require all your firmness to communicate it to Lady Margaret. Mr Perceval going into the House of Commons was shot by a villain, in the breast; & is since dead. Indeed he lived but a very short time after the blow. Mrs Perceval is informed, & is as well as can be expected. Lord Arden is here . . [*18*]

The shock was the greater because Jane's marriage with Perceval had been and remained a love-match. They had been denied the approval of her father, Sir Thomas Wilson, who had been quite happy to see another daughter, Margaretta Elizabeth, married to Perceval's elder brother Lord Arden, but did not welcome as son-in-law an impecunious lawyer; Perceval, as the second son of a second marriage of his father, the Earl of Egmont, appeared to have no prospects either of title or of fortune. The young couple had therefore patiently waited for Jane's twenty-first birthday in July 1790; a month later, they were secretly wed, the bride attired in her riding habit. The marriage had been particularly happy, had eventually won over the disapproving Sir Thomas, and had produced thirteen children, of whom eleven were living at the time of the tragedy.

A footnote to the horror was added when it was discovered that one of Perceval's young sons (the eldest was now only seventeen) had by chance dropped in to visit Parliament that afternoon. 'We saw a boy in the House, under the gallery, in great affliction, whom we suppose to be the unfortunate youth,' reported the *Liverpool Mercury*'s 15 May issue, reprinting from the *Globe Paper* of the 12th.

At one o'clock on the morning of Tuesday, 12 May, Lord Arden and the Speaker, Charles Abbot, accompanied the body of the Prime Minister to No. 10, Downing Street, where Jane Perceval lay in a state of dry-eyed shock behind the drawn window-blinds. And at one o'clock the dazed and weary Cabinet members, in almost the same state of shock, adjourned to make their way home, forced in some cases by hissing and hostile crowds to detour via Abingdon Street.

While the victim's body lay in what had been his dressing-room, surrounded by lighted wax candles and attended by two of the household servants, reporters were dashing all over London, buttonholing everyone who could contribute an anecdote, stitching together all the fragments of information into a patchwork fabric of fact, fiction and hearsay, about the man John Bellingham (*Billingham* ? – *George* Bellingham – John *James* Bellingham ? – John *Charles* Bellingham?) who had perpetrated this incredible and seemingly senseless act.

The nature of the man's claims [said the *Morning Chronicle* next morning] we understand to be no other than that he imputes to our Ministers in Russia the want of protection, or of interference in a dispute which he had with the Consul of

Archangel, by which he incurred a loss of seven or 8,000 *l*, but in which the British Government had nothing to do. He was imprisoned in Russia in consequence of his violence; and on his arrival here, he applied to all the public offices, even those which had nothing to do with any such business; and was told by all of them, that they could not take cognizance of his private affairs. He says that he was driven to despair; he three weeks ago, bought the pistols for the horrid deed, which he has at last perpetrated.

Sir William Curtis, a London Member of Parliament, recalled that Bellingham had told him, 'I have been fourteen days in making my mind up to the deed, but never could accomplish it until this moment.' Dowling remembered that Bellingham had actually sat next to him in the gallery during the past week, and talked to him; about two weeks earlier, he had asked to have Mr Secretary Ryder pointed out to him. Several people had seen him about the House of Commons over the past few weeks, especially near the door commanding a view of the Treasury bench, looking through his opera glass and asking for identification of the ministers. He had frequently dined in the coffee-room.

Jane Perceval's dazed and stony calm had been worrying her family and her friends. Next morning she was taken to the candle-lit room where her husband's body lay; she burst into uncontrollable tears. Perceval's expression in death retained the sweetness that was remarked on by many of his colleagues. 'Nothing could be more calm and undisturbed than his countenance is,' wrote one grieving sister, Lady Redesdale, to another, Margaret Walpole [19].

The body was viewed the same morning by the coroner's jury. An inquest was called for eleven o'clock by the coroner for Westminster, Anthony Gell, and held at The Rose and Crown, Downing Street, a public house owned by Francis Dukes.* With Mr Gell,

---

* Some of the newspapers named The Cat and Bagpipes, Downing Street, as the location of the inquest. It is an odd fact that nowhere in the parish of St Margaret's (or the parish of St John the Evangelist) is a public house of this name listed for 1812. The house owned by Francis Dukes had been The Rose and Crown, at the same address, since 1800 at least (G.L.R.O./ W.L.V.R., 1812). The Rose and Crown, the house of Francis Dukes, is the name given on the coroner's report (G.L.R.O./O.B./S.R., 13 May 1812).

the twenty-one jurors, all householders of the parish of St Margaret's, 'good and lawful men . . . duly chosen', walked the few paces to the late Prime Minister's house. The street was crowded with curious spectators, though police officers had been stationed at its entrance to try to keep it clear for residents and people with business in the area. After viewing the body for ten minutes, the jurors returned to The Rose and Crown and proceeded to hear the witnesses, Henry Burgess, Isaac Gascoyne, Joseph Hume, William Smith and Surgeon William Lynn.

The evidence, though somewhat amplified, was largely the same as that given the night before. With military fervour, General Gascoyne added some dash and drama to his account:

> I sprung upon him, and grasped him by the breast and neck; I perceived him raising his left hand with a pistol in it; I let go my hold, and seized his wrist with both hands, and twisted his arm round with all my force; he seemed to have little hold of the pistol; I desired a person standing by to take the pistol from his hand, which was done. I took papers from his pocket, and tied them up; he appeared to be dragging from my hold, but I kept him fast.

He added that Bellingham had called at his home in Hertford Street, Mayfair, about three weeks earlier, and, as one of the general's constituents, had asked for parliamentary assistance for his cause, which Gascoyne had not felt able to give him.

Joseph Hume's evidence was also graphic: he offered a vivid picture of the fury with which the prisoner had been apprehended.

> [Bellingham] appeared to be forcibly pulled, on every side, by the bye-standers; appeared to suffer considerably from the force used by such bye-standers; appeared considerably agitated, and in the act of disengaging his hand from the person who grasped it severely. I seized his left arm at the moment that General Gascoyne was pulling from the person of the prisoner a bundle of papers; one of the General's hands being occupied grasping the prisoner, I seized hold of the papers from the General's right hand, informing him that I would take care of them; I still retained hold of the prisoner, and saw a person in the act of pulling from about the waist of the

prisoner a small pocket steel pistol, which he immediately examined, and found primed; I desired that person to take care of it, and on subsequent examination, I found that same pistol to contain a ball and powder.

Hume threw in a comment about Bellingham's apparent mental state. 'On the whole, I do consider that he was perfectly sane, making a little allowance for the agitation of the moment.'

After William Smith had repeated his earlier evidence, and Dr Lynn had recorded the medical details of Perceval's death, a verdict of wilful murder was returned.

> . . . John Bellingham alias John Billingham not having the fear of God before his Eyes but moved and seduced by the Instigation of the Devil . . . in and upon the said Spencer Perceval . . . did make an Assault [with] a certain Pistol of the value of nine shillings charged and loaded with Gunpowder and a Leaden Bullet, which he . . . then and there had and held in his right hand to and against the Breast of him the said Spencer Perceval [and] did then and there shoot off and discharge . . . and of his Malice aforethought did then and there give unto him the said Spencer Perceval with the leaden Bullet aforesaid . . . shot off and discharged out of the Pistol aforesaid by the force of the Gunpowder aforesaid in upon and through the Breast of him the said Spencer Perceval one Mortal Wound . . .[20].

The Prime Minister's Private Secretary, Thomas Constantine Brooksbank, who lived in Hans Place, Chelsea, was thereupon bound over in forty pounds recognizance to prefer a bill of indictment against John Bellingham, alias John Billingham.

Apprehensions of conspiracy had been quieted fairly quickly, as no signs of great country-wide upheaval had appeared. By Wednesday this realization had comfortably cheered the *Morning Chronicle*. 'It indeed afforded some relief to the agitated feelings of the community to find, that the assassin was neither a Roman Catholic nor a Manufacturer – that he had nothing to do with the Orders in Council – and was not a Reformer of Political Abuses.' In fact, although the crowds in the city were large and noisy and excited, and roamed the streets until late, it was soon realized that military precautions could be somewhat relaxed. By three o'clock on Tuesday morning, indeed, as no sign of trouble had developed in the area, the Duke of Sussex had regaled 'with his usual hospitality' his Royal North Britons, who had been patiently standing around in Gray's Inn gardens for the past six hours, gave them 'an impressive address', and packed them off home [21].

While the speculations about Bellingham's sanity flew from tongue to tongue, and anxieties were building up about his motives and his possible accomplices, and the bewildered Government gathered itself together to cope with the effects of the shock waves rippling across the country, the assassin – relaxed, courteous, and composed – slept peacefully on the barrack bed in his cell at Newgate. At seven o'clock on Tuesday he awoke, refreshed, and sent for breakfast; for fear of possible poison, Keeper Newman himself prepared a large basin of sweetened tea, with two buttered rolls, which Bellingham ate with a good appetite, cheerfully conversing with his attendants. He had been born at St Neots in Huntingdonshire, he told them, according to the newspaper reports; he had a wife and three children in Liverpool.

When Mr Alderman Combe and other magistrates called on him during the day, he conversed pleasantly, and answered their questions with a reserved dignity, raising some of his own. He asked what direction the ball had taken when entering Perceval's breast, and when told that the downward slant of its path had caused speculation that he had had to fire over the shoulder of a person standing between himself and his victim, he was shocked. Never would he have dreamed of firing, and thus endangering a bystander, he exclaimed, had Perceval not been immediately before him and his aim unobstructed.

A gentleman giving his name as Hokkirk inquired for him at the prison during the day, but was not allowed to visit his cell. Hokkirk told interrogators that Bellingham's father had died mad, and that he knew Bellingham himself to be deranged. But in a day when signs of delusion had to be more apparent to a jury than those Bellingham exhibited, his calm demeanour showed nothing that would be accepted as madness: almost the opposite. The *Courier* commented on 13 May:

It was at first taken for granted, for it was impossible to believe such an act could be perpetrated by any other than an

insane man, that the man laboured under insanity, but it
would be difficult to come to this conclusion from the manner
and demeanour of the prisoner. We do not mean his manner
at the time of committing the murder, but his conduct before
and after. He has transacted business with his Solicitor and
many others within a week past, and nothing appeared in his
conduct to induce a suspicion of his labouring under insanity.
He has since been very much employed in writing, and there
is nothing of that hurry in his action, or want of method in
his style, to induce us to believe, that he does now or has ever
laboured under mental derangement.

There was, in fact, never to appear any glimmer of remorse or
guilt for what he had done. He had made application to every
person likely to procure him redress, he explained with an air of
patient reason, as to obtuse children, and he had been at length
driven to despair by being told at the public offices that he could
expect no aid, but might do his worst. What was this but official
permission to do whatever he thought necessary to bring his case
before the public? If he had to kill someone (or only wound someone, which he indicated would have served his purpose as well),
was this not a necessary next step forced on him – even suggested
to him – by the authorities?

During the morning he called for pen and paper, and wrote
letters: to his wife, telling her what he had done (though he added
the somewhat redundant comment that she would probably have
heard already), and to a friend in Liverpool. It was remarked how
neatly he prepared the letters; both were sent for censorship to
the Secretary of State. To his landlady (the Press called her
'Rebecca Roberts', though she signed her name 'Robarts' on her
receipts for his rent) he directed a request for some personal belongings to be sent to Newgate.

Tuesday morning, Old Bailey

Dear Madam,

Yesterday midnight I was escorted to this neighbourhood
by a noble troop of light horse, and delivered into the care
of Mr Newman (by Mr Taylor, the magistrate and M.P.) as
a State Prisoner of the first class. For eight years I have never

found my mind so tranquil as since this melancholy, but necessary catastrophe: as the merits or demerits of my peculiar case must be regularly unfolded in a Criminal Court of Justice to ascertain the guilty party, by a jury of my country, I have to request the favour of you to send me three or four shirts, some cravats, handkerchiefs, night-caps, stockings, &c. out of my drawers, together with comb, soap, toothbrush, with any other trifle that presents itself which you think I may have occasion for, and inclose them in my leather trunk, and the key please to send sealed, per bearer; also my great coat, flannel gown, and black waistcoat, which will much oblige, Dear Madam, your very obedient Servant,

JOHN BELLINGHAM

To the above please to add the prayer book.

He announced cheerfully that he did not expect to be tried during the present sessions, which were to begin on the morrow, Wednesday, 13 May, as he would not have sufficient time to prepare a defence and produce witnesses.

It is difficult to account for the composure and serenity in which this unhappy criminal passes his time [marvelled the *Sun* on the 14th]. If the worm of conscience were gnawing him within, he could not sleep with such regularity and soundness, nor demean himself with such ease, if not cheerfulness, as he appears to do. He has frequently declared, most solemnly, since he has been in Newgate, that he had no malice to Mr Perceval, and that if Lord G. L. Gower or Mr Ryder had first appeared before him, he would have fixed upon either.

CHAPTER FOUR

The man, not the minister

THE shock of the previous day's tragedy brought Members crowding into both Houses of Parliament for Tuesday's sittings. In the House of Lords at five o'clock the Earl of Liverpool presented the Prince Regent's message, which expressed his desire that provision should be made for Perceval's wife and family. Reading it, the Lord Chancellor was so affected by emotion that he had great difficulty in finishing. The horror of the murder still bound them all, so that everyone shrank from any mention of political differences. Earl Grey diffidently suggested that he would have liked to see unanimity reached after longer deliberation, but that he agreed wholeheartedly with the sentiment and purpose of the Regent's wishes. An address of concurrence was moved at once, and carried without dissent.

More than four hundred and fifty Members had crammed the benches of the House of Commons when that House met at four o'clock in an impressive display of concern and sympathy. 'Every seat, both in the body and in the galleries, was crowded to excess.' The entrance of the Speaker brought everyone to his feet, all standing in silence with bared heads until the chaplain was called, when they knelt to join in the prayers.

Lord Castlereagh presented the Prince Regent's message, which was read by the Speaker. Then, in place of Richard Ryder, who was still too shocked by the loss of his friend to be able to speak without breaking down, Castlereagh moved an address to the Regent, agreed by all, that the House 'shall feel it a grateful act of public duty, under the melancholy circumstances of this afflicting case, to enable His Royal Highness, in the name and on the behalf of His Majesty, to make such provision for the Widow and Family of the Right honourable *Spencer Perceval*, as may be consistent with the justice and the liberality of Parliament'. A proposal that the address should be presented only by those who were Members of the Privy Council was shot down in favour of presentation by the whole House when the Regent should indicate a time for receiving them.

'By common consent, no other business was done. Lord Castlereagh presented the Message, and moved the Address. In most faces there was an agony of tears; and neither Lord Castlereagh, Ponsonby, Whitbread, nor Canning could give a dry utterance to their sentiments' [22].

Some public comfort was derived from the relevation that the last few days of Perceval's life had been peculiarly happy. The diary of his friend Robert Plumer Ward tells of charmingly simple dinners throughout the preceding months, at which up to a dozen guests might join the family, when 'Perceval was never more easy or more cheerful.' Miss Perceval (Jane, the eldest child) had told Ward only five weeks earlier that the young people had begged their father to give a ball, and he had promised to do so *when he had made a general peace which the whole nation should approve*'. His eldest son and namesake was to take part in the speech-day activities at Harrow within the next few days; and on the previous Sunday, at St Martin-in-the-Fields, he had seen his daughters confirmed by the Bishop of London [23].

Preparing to dress on Sunday, 10 May, the day before his death, Perceval had asked his valet about his engagements for the day, and was delighted to find there were none.

'What, not anyone to dinner? Then I am happy, for I shall have a pleasure I very seldom enjoy, of dining with my family alone' [24].

After family prayers that night, he had begged Jane to allow the children to linger before going up to bed, and kissed them all as they gathered around him. His final meal on the fatal day itself had been a quiet family dinner at two thirty.

As the immediate shock wore off, Members of Parliament who now found they had come under the scrutiny of Bellingham's opera glasses during the preceding weeks – Ryder and other Ministers – may have shivered a bit at narrow escapes. Certainly Lord Chancellor Eldon did, confiding to his Anecdote Book the 'most providential escape' he thought he might have experienced by having passed the assassin in the lobby wearing the coat and hat he had borrowed from an attendant in which to take a walk before going into the House of Lords [25].

Debate on a suitable provision for Perceval's family was held at length on Wednesday. 'Poor Perceval,' mused the diplomat Sir George Jackson. 'Poor in every sense, I believe; for he was too honest to enrich himself, however he may have helped to enrich others. He has left a widow and a family of twelve children; they say, most scantily provided for' [26].

That some provision should be made was agreed by all. It remained only to decide the amount. Perceval had written a simple will about four years ago, on a half-sheet of paper, and had handed a copy to his wife only six weeks earlier. He had left everything to Jane – 'all his freeholds, copy holds, and other estates, in reversion, expectancy, or remainder' [27]. But as the second son of a second marriage, even though his father was an earl, Perceval's expectation of any great inheritance was small. As well, as his friends were quick to point out, he had forgone the possibility of earning a large fortune in the practice of law by entering politics. The Member for Surrey, Mr Holme Sumner, cried in the House that Wednesday:

Had he not, for the service of his country, deserted the service of his family, at a time when he had attained the loftiest eminence in the law . . . he might have died possessed of a large fortune. He held the high office of Attorney-General, and had a vacancy occurred, he would have been exalted to the high station of a Chief Justice or a Chancellor – (hear) – Was it to be believed, that in such a case the situation of his family would not have been incomparably more affluent than under the present circumstances he had left them? [28]

In the shock of recent events, every Member was doing his best to subdue party feeling. Sir Francis Burdett earned particular commendation from the Press in view of his known opposition to Perceval, by rising to place on record 'as strongly as any man' his concurrence 'in the fullness of lamentation and abhorrence of the most atrocious deed committed within these walls' [29]. The linking of his name with the crowd's applause for Bellingham had made necessary a public dissociation from any approval of the act, and he pleaded that the address to the Regent should be a simple and unanimous statement of grief.

William Wilberforce, the Member for Bramber in Sussex, who had been a close friend of Perceval for thirty-five years, paid tribute to his character. 'A man of more real sweetness of temper; a man more highly blest by nature, was never known, or one in whom goodness of disposition was more deeply rooted.' Wilberforce had been standing in the front room of Thomas Babington's house in Downing Street when Perceval had hurried by on his last walk to the Parliament Buildings, and, at the time, the sight of the slight Prime Minister had started him on a eulogy of his friend's good qualities as he turned away from the window to the group gathered in the room. In the present debate, he too pleaded for a unanimous vote that would recognize the sincerity of the Prime Minister's motives, even though there might be disagreement with his policies. 'The family would doubtless be much more highly gratified in obtaining a smaller, frank, warm, and unanimous vote, than in receiving a larger amount, which might be deemed, even by a few, unnecessary and improper extravagance' [30].

The proposal was for a sum of £50,000 to be divided among the younger children, with an annuity of £2,000 for Mrs Perceval. An amendment deplored by many Members suggested an equal annuity for the eldest son. The House eventually voted an annuity of £2,000 to Jane, payable after her death to her husband's heir, whether son or grandson; of £1,000 to such heir up to the time of Jane's death, when her annuity would revert to him; and of £50,000, tax free, 'to be vested in Trustees for the use of the twelve Children of the late Right Honourable *Spencer Perceval* . . .' The Act of 9 June was made retroactive to the day of the assassination [31].

Partisan comment following the decision on the amount was

sometimes cynical, more often passionate and uninhibited: some deplored any award at all, others its parsimony. One critic decried provision to a widow who, 'allied to the first and most opulent families in the kingdom, and thus nobly as well as powerfully connected, has abundant means of providing for her fatherless progeny'. Leigh Hunt, in the *Examiner*, also disapproved: 'A Minister's family consisting of a lady and twelve children in possession of nearly 7,000 *l.* a year, must be presumed as capable of procuring the latter good education as that of a country gentleman in similar circumstances' [32].

The *Courier* was loudly ashamed.

The intended provision for Mr Perceval's family has disappointed us, and from its smallness, is utterly unworthy the national character – a sum totally insufficient to educate and maintain them in the rank they deserve to occupy – insufficient even to set them up in any trade! This is the allowance which the liberality and justice of the nation are called upon to give to the family of a man at the head of the Administration of the Country, cut off in the exercise of his duty, and leaving his children to that nation in whose service he had lost his valuable life ... Is it to propitiate the populace that the provision has been so small? ... The family may be contented with what is proposed, for they could hardly be expected to chaffer and haggle about the value of a father and a husband's life – 'a pound of flesh' against so much pension ... The whole should have been done by Parliament upon a great scale [33].

Remnants of the provision, which later generations of the family would cheerfully dub 'murder money', were still providing opportunities for education to grandchildren and great-grandchildren a hundred-odd years later [34].

Other help was offered the stricken family. Early in June, Jane Perceval was asked by the Honourable Society of Lincoln's Inn to nominate two of her sons to occupy chambers now vacant, the cost of their legal education to be met by the benchers. She chose the eldest, Spencer, and her eighth child and fifth son, Dudley. It was kindly added that this offer did not obligate the boys to follow the profession of law if they later decided against it Early in the following year, Spencer was also given the tellership of the Exchequer [35].

Memorial sermons were preached across the nation, in London, Nottinghamshire, Durham, Wiltshire. The Reverend John Batchellor, vicar of Chitterne in Wiltshire, admitting that his sermon was 'chiefly taken from Dr Ogden's collection, except where it is adapted to the mournful case that is the subject of it', nevertheless published and sold it for a shilling. A great deal of bad verse appeared ('1/6d, neatly printed'), with unmemorable lines like 'Tho' now he slumbers in the dreary tomb / Soon shall he rise unsullied from the dust,' and 'Assassin! direst fiend of Hell! / How thou has triumph'd England's sorrows tell!' There were also less high-flown efforts, verse with a sting in its tail:

> In the dirge we sung o'er thee no censure was heard,
>   Unembitter'd and free did the tear-drop descend;
> We forgot, in that hour, how the statesman had err'd,
>   And wept for the father, the husband, and friend!...
>
> Even now, if a selfish emotion intrude,
>   'Tis to wish thou had'st chosen some lowlier state –
> Had'st known what thou wert – and content to be good,
>   Had'st ne'er, for our ruin, aspir'd to be *great*' [36].

In Northampton, where the shock was felt with particular horror, as Perceval had been for sixteen years the Member for the borough, and deputy town recorder for twenty-one years, the grieving inhabitants voted to wear mourning for a fortnight. Someone signing himself 'Observer' got off a prompt suggestion to the *Public Ledger* for a full month of voluntary mourning dress right across the country, to express national sorrow and indignation [37].

Addresses to the Prince Regent poured in from the four corners of the kingdom; the papers were filled with advertisements announcing public meetings to consider such addresses. They came, filled with fervent patriotism, from the Freeholders of the County of Northampton; the Inhabitants of the City of Bristol; the Magistracy of Middlesex; the Vestry of St-Mary-le-bonne; the County of Surrey; the Freeholders, Justices of the Peace and the Commissioners of Supply in the Shire of Perth; the Corporation of Derby;

the Corporation and City of York. The Court of the Lord Mayor and Aldermen of the City of London got off the mark quickly, at a meeting on the morning of the assassination. The Court of Common Council (London) debated their address on Saturday, 16 May, though the wording was subsequently queried in the best tradition by Robert Waithman, the Town Clerk, who thought that 'motives most pure' sounded better than 'patriotism most ardent'. He was overruled 'after some discussion' not difficult to imagine. A somewhat similar splitting of hairs occurred at Cambridge, where addresses prepared by the Bishop of Bristol and the Vice-Chancellor, Dr Brown, were both thrown out when neither would accept the version of the other. 'The puny politics of the University,' remarked *The Times* caustically [38].

The City of Liverpool, especially sensitive to its unenviable reputation as the residence of the assassin and his family, rushed to deposit its loyal address at most of the public places in the town so that an impressive total of signatures might bury the stain. 'An Englishman', who protested its wording as an unnecessary endorsement of Perceval the Minister, summed up an attitude that – now the first shock was wearing off – had begun to seep through in speeches and editorials. He wrote in the *Liverpool Mercury* of 22 May:

I am well convinced that many persons have withheld their names, from a perusal of the latter part. Had this Address been confined to the natural expression of satisfaction at being able with truth to disclaim the assassin as a townsman; or, of those *'feelings of unmixed indignation, with which, in common with every British subject, we contemplate one of the most atrocious acts which have ever disgraced the annals of our history'*, I have no doubt that the signatures would have been much more numerous; but when we are called upon, in the same breath, to *'express our admiration at the lofty devotion of mind, and firm integrity of principle of the deceased'*, I for one am compelled to hesitate: for when I contemplate the projectors of the Copenhagen expedition – that wholesale murder – that foul and indelible stain on our country: – when I further reflect on the systematic opposition shewn to Reform, to every scheme of public economy, and to Catholic emancipation, upon which the safety, and perhaps the very existence of our country, depend – I cannot but conclude, that this *'lofty elevation of mind'*, this *'firm integrity of principle'*, have been intirely confined to the sphere of *private life* . . .

For the short period during which the whole nation was in shock, normal reactions were frozen, as it were, into a kind of static inability to see beyond the fact of Perceval's sudden non-existence. Bellingham's own insistence that he had shot the minister, not the man, operated in reverse within the Government for this space of time. For those traumatic hours when the shadow of the Prime Minister's death was the only reality, the Members almost forgot the minister in their distress over the death of the man, their colleague; who, despite political differences – often differences expressed with violence – was universally liked by those who knew him. Samuel Whitbread, for instance, protested earnestly that though he might disagree implacably with his policies, 'having throughout been a marked and determined political antagonist of the Right Honourable Gentleman', he could not maintain any such feelings of resentment or displeasure outside the House. Indeed, 'against the Right Honourable Gentleman, he had ever found it impossible to carry such a feeling even so far as the door' [39].

Among many – though not all – of the 'lower orders', who did not know the man, but knew his policies and blamed them for the miseries of poverty and hardship in their own lives, the effect of the news was different. Large sections of the crowd around Westminster had been hostile. The London Press was horrified to report how some of the disaffected centres in the country had received the news of the assassination. The *Nottingham Journal* published a shamefaced account of what happened there on the night of Tuesday, 12 May.

We are sorry to observe that a strong disposition to tumult prevailed in this town on Tuesday evening last. As soon as the truth of the report respecting the murder of Mr Perceval had been ascertained, a few deluded men and ignorant boys, who had been taught to believe that that gentleman was the prime cause of all our commercial distresses, and sufferings among the people, at the present time, assembled in the neighbourhood of Fisher Gate, and proceeded with a band of music all through the principal streets. They were soon joined by a numerous rabble, who, in the most indecent and reprehensible manner, testified their joy at the horrid catastrophe, by repeated shouts, the firing of guns, and every species of exultation. In this manner they continued to parade the streets for nearly two hours, to the great annoyance of the peaceable and well-disposed part of the community. It was at length deemed advisable by those to whose charge the preservation of the public peace is committed, to order out the military, and to read the Riot Act; but the mob shortly afterwards began to disperse, which rendered the use of force unnecessary. A strong military piquet, however, was kept up all night.

On Wednesday evening, about dusk, a multitude again collected, seemingly with the design of renewing the uproar, and insulting the Magistracy and soldiery, but no attempt at violence was offered, and the night passed over quietly. The town has since remained perfectly peaceable.

The above circumstances exhibit a melancholy proof of the infatuation and depravity which reigns amongst many of the lower orders [wrote the editors from out of their sackcloth and ashes]. We could not have believed that an Englishman (naturally humane) could be found whose mind was so poisoned by the gangrene of prejudice, as to openly applaud a deed so dark, so foul, the very contemplation of which makes humanity shudder! It has been reserved, however, (and we blush to name it!) for the town of Nottingham alone to display this spirit – a spirit to which no epithet, however severe, can be applied to mark its infamy, and which merits the execration of every good man, of whatever principle, throughout the land. We may indeed exclaim, 'O tempora! O mores!'

At least, the *Journal* was able to report thankfully a week later, the ringing of bells at St Peter's Church that night had not been connected with this deplorable public rejoicing. It simply happened to be the regular night for the bell-ringers to practise.

CHAPTER FIVE

A true Bill against John Bellingham

It had been rumoured that the violence in word and deed in some quarters of the kingdom might intimidate the Regent to the extent of causing a change in Government – a suggestion scornfully dismissed by the *Courier*. 'The Prince is all a Brunswick, as the Opposition will find' [*40*].

Not everyone agreed. 'I think the Regent will be a good deal frightened,' wrote the Honourable Mrs Calvert in her diary on 12 May, 'and he is a nervous man. It is said the populace said last night, "Perceval is down, and the Regent must be down next."' On the 15th, Mrs Calvert was shocked by the 'printed placards put on the House of Commons yesterday stating that Mr Perceval's ribs were only fit to broil the Regent's heart on. How horrible!' [*41*]

On 20 May, Georgiana Lady Spencer was writing anxiously to her daughter Lady Bessborough, 'Is it true that the Prince has had a threatening letter bidding him beware of the same fate [as] Mr Percival has had?' He had, in fact, received two such letters. The first, from 'Vox Populi', was addressed to his secretary, Colonel John McMahon.

'Provisions cheaper – *Bread or Blood* – Tell your Master he is a *Damn'd unfeeling Scoundrel*, and if he don't attend to the above, *Death* shall be his portion, & that soon, it's come to the point now, & we are determined to strike the decisive blow.'

The second came to the Prince himself, at Windsor:

George Prince of Wales. Take care of yourself, for your Life is in danger, you shall meet the same fate as Mr Perceval if Billenghall is *hung before this reach you*. You blackguard you shall be shot before three months is *elapsed* if Billenghall is hung you shall be shot as sure as
    I remain an Enemy of all the damned Royal Family [42].

To the disgust of the *Morning Chronicle*, a reward of one thousand pounds was offered for the arrest and conviction of the culprits. 'We are sorry to see that any notice has been taken of such contemptible trash as the above ... None but the basest of the human race are guilty of anonymous threats, and every man of sense treats them with contempt.' On 27 May the *Chronicle* claimed to have identified the writer, an insane person with a record of making wild threats. Others in high places were also receiving unpleasant letters: they should be treated with silent contempt, thought the *Chronicle*, 'for there is nothing more certain [than] that they who would use daggers do not speak daggers' [43].
    An incautious and unlucky seaman named Abraham King on board the eighty-gun Royal Navy ship *Tonnant* in Cawsand Bay got himself into trouble by copying Bellingham's letter to the Bow Street magistrates with relevant substitutions, and sending it to an unpopular captain. It earned him three hundred lashes and a flogging through the fleet [44].
    These were, however, fairly isolated incidents. Though the assassination had touched off some minor violence, it was soon clear that no organized rebellion was afoot. Sporadic unrest persisted, and some advantage was taken of the crisis by disaffected souls, but this was largely letting off steam. What now became important was the matter of a new Government.
    The assassination 'immediately set in motion all that mass of political intrigue and speculation which never fails to be called

into activity upon a prospect of change in the government', said the *Annual Register* [45]. The Whigs saw the event as an opportunity for the Prince Regent to bring them to power at last; but the Regent soon made it clear that his former friends need hold to no such expectation. Everyone at once began jockeying for position.

The Cabinet Council had been meeting every night since Perceval's murder. After a meeting held on Tuesday the 12th in the Home Secretary's office, the Lord Chancellor, Castlereagh and Richard Ryder had gone to the Regent to make some kind of interim arrangement until a successor to Perceval could be appointed [46].

'Lord Liverpool was Premier for *one* day and Mr Vansittart Chancellor of the Exchequer,' said Mrs Calvert's diary with keen interest on 25 May, 'but they resigned in consequence of an address from Parliament; moved by Mr Stuart Wortley, and carried by a majority of four to the Regent to appoint a more efficient Ministry' [47]. Overtures were made, without success, to Lord Wellesley and George Canning to join the administration; but 'Wellesley and Canning have created a demur by insisting on the Catholic claims being conceded. The Prince says he cannot consent to this point during his father's life.' The offer of a coalition with the Whigs was refused by Lords Grey and Grenville. Lord Moira presented a programme that might have united the various factions, but could not persuade them into final agreement.

A London correspondent gave a neat summary in the *Edinburgh Weekly Journal*:

> Upon the interesting subject of the arrangement of a Government, we have little to communicate, since nothing is known but the number of interviews this Earl has had with that Marquis, and this Lord with that Duke; from a knowledge of which facts, however, our politicians exert their art of divination, and hazard conjectures, which do more credit to their invention than to their sagacity . . . The truth, we believe, is, that nothing is yet determined, and every man's wish is father to his thoughts upon the subject [48].

Unperturbed by the upheaval he had caused, and caring nothing for ministerial dilemmas, John Bellingham continued to pass his days placidly in Newgate. Two days after the assassination, on Wednesday, 13 May, the *Courier* was one of the papers able to present its readers with a fairly comprehensive account of Bellingham's life. This was to prove inaccurate in some particulars, but at least it gave form and substance to the background of a man whose past and whose reasons for an incomprehensible act everyone wanted to know. In the light of the fears everyone had had that the assassin might be the agent of some dreadful conspiracy about to inflame the whole country, it was some comfort to find him reduced to the dimensions of a man with a private grievance.

'The poor wretch seems to have been driven to madness by hard usage inflicted upon him by the brutal despotism of Russia,' wrote the Honourable John Ward compassionately to his Ivy [49].

Along with the infiltrations by which it appeared he had been attempting to breach the various Government departments, Bellingham had hoped to have his case given a national hearing through the House of Commons. He had, accordingly, presented a petition dated 28 February to the Prince Regent, with a request that it be brought to the attention of Parliament. Having been refused this approach, he had paid £9 15s. 0d. to A. Macpherson, a Covent Garden printer, for 660 copies of a covering letter dated 12 March to go to all Members, together with copies of the rejected petition. No one had taken any notice of it at the time, when he had been handing them to Members; but by Wednesday after the assassination, most of the daily papers had got hold of copies, and presented either the full text or summarized versions [50].

At seven o'clock that morning, Bellingham woke from a sound sleep and ate a light breakfast at nine, chatting amicably with the keepers. He turned the pages of the morning paper, and remarked delightedly that his memorial had been printed.

'My memorial then has, at last, gone forth to the world; the public will now be able to judge my case, and do me the justice to say, I have only done my duty.' Sharply warned by the keepers to watch his language, he expressed indifference to what might happen to him. He was doing little brooding about either his appalling act, or his unhappy past, so confident was he that he had taken the only step left to him for the righting of his wrongs. 'They can do me no harm,' he had told the keepers, 'but the government has cause for fear' [51].

During the morning he was visited by both the sheriffs, with other gentlemen, with whom he conversed calmly except on the subject of the assassination. On this, he became vehement, insisting that he would be vindicated at his trial, when people would learn how far a minister was justified in refusing justice to an injured individual. He had shot the minister, not the man, he stated again; he would have been worse than a brute, he said, if the deed had been committed from personal malice.

After two hours with his solicitor, James Harmer, when he expressed a desire to have Henry Brougham and Peter Alley appointed counsel for his defence, he dined well at two o'clock on 'roast beef and potatoes, with beer, but no wine, though he might have had some if he wished'. His dinner was somewhat interrupted by the comings and goings of various people, including an old schoolmate named Fidler, with whom he was allowed to chat for a while in the turnkey's presence. He had by now received some of his personal belongings from Mrs Robarts, and was observed from time to time studying the prayer book, especially (it was noted) the Psalms [52].

The daily papers continued aghast at the contrast between the unthinkable horror of the deed he had committed and the demeanour he presented both before the act and afterwards in Newgate. Opinion swung in a circle of confusion. He must have been insane to have done such a thing! But how then could the sanity in every other area of his life be explained?

Even his handwriting spoke of sanity – 'a fine mercantile hand' – careful, painstaking and even, described by another contemporary writer as 'clerkly'; it was, perhaps, the writing one would expect from a man whose stubborn assurance would stand unmoved by any argument of logic. Allowing for the rather verbose and long-winded style of the day, all Bellingham's petitions and statements of his case were remarkably lucid and literate.

On Thursday afternoon, in stately ceremonial, both Houses of Parliament and the Corporation of the City of London presented their addresses to the Prince Regent, who, attended by the ministers of State, the Lord Steward, the Lord Chamberlain, the Groom of the Stole, Gold Stick and other dignitaries, received them on his throne in 'the great gilt saloon' at Carlton House. The Peers met in the House at half past one, the elected Members in the House of Commons at two, in full Court suits of mourning; those in regimentals or naval uniform wore black armbands. A solemn procession of carriages – nearly two hundred – accompanied the addresses, which were received in sequence, and answered with a proper dignity.

At four, another splendid procession arrived at Carlton House. The Lord Mayor, his carriage drawn by six horses (not the State Coach, which was under repair at the time), was attended with proper formality by the Recorder, the sheriffs, the Remembrancer, the Town Clerk, the Mace, the Sword of State, the City marshals and seventeen aldermen. The Recorder, John Sylvester, read the address; after which, 'They were all most graciously received, and had the honour to kiss the Prince's hand' [53].

That morning, the due processes of law had taken another step forward when the Grand Jury – foreman David Owen, merchant, of No. 7, Norfolk Street, Strand, with twenty-two substantial citizens of varying occupations (apothecary, wine merchant, glover, optician, jeweller, bookseller, lace-maker, manufacturer of flageolets) – met at the Sessions House, Clerkenwell. Here those witnesses who had already appeared twice before were heard again. A Mr Boys (probably the Margate solicitor) added his verdict as another eye-witness, brought to the hearing by Sir Edward Knatchbull after the latter had observed him in a coffee-house drawing a plan of the lobby and explaining how near he had been standing to the assassin. Following a short deliberation, the jury proceeded to the Court of Oyer and Terminer at Justice Hall in the Old Bailey, and declared before upwards of twenty magistrates that they had found a 'true Bill against John Bellingham, for the wilful murder of the Right Honourable Spencer Perceval' [54].

Bellingham now stood under a double indictment, and it was decided to hold his trial the next day, Friday the 15th. In an unprecedented action, the Solicitor for the Treasury, the Honourable Charles Litchfield, made a personal visit to Newgate to tell him of the decision. Bellingham probably thought it no more than his due.

He was not seriously disturbed. When a Liverpool friend in London on business, Mary Stevens, was permitted to visit him later, just before she left to return home, he did not take advantage of the opportunity to write to his wife. 'He would rather wait till the next day, that he might acquaint her with his liberation, which he confidently anticipated before the going out of the post.' While Miss Stevens was with him, it was reported that he received a small box containing bank notes for fifty pounds, twenty pounds, and small sums, to an approximate total of a hundred guineas. Its donor remained a mystery; perhaps, the journals surmised, a gift from some unknown friend towards the cost of the trial [55].

He had risen at seven as usual on Thursday morning, 'obviously refreshed and apparently unaffected by the unfortunate circumstances of his situation', and breakfasted at eight thirty. Most of the morning was spent pensively (and awkwardly, because of his fetters) walking to and fro, occasionally pondering the prayer book. At two, his dinner consisted of minced veal and potatoes and a pint of porter. Harmer, his solicitor, called again between four and five o'clock, but Bellingham had evidently decided he was competent to manage his own business, and refused further discussion. At six o'clock, after drinking some tea, he settled to the task of mapping out his defence, and wrote steadily until shortly before nine. Running out of paper, he made a request to Newman, the Keeper of Newgate, for a fresh supply, which was granted, and a few glasses of wine, which was not.

At this point, his trunk was removed in accordance with some obscure prison regulation, though he kept the key, and was allowed also to retain his dressing-gown. A little after nine he was served with a glass of porter, and returned with absorption to his writing. At midnight, he asked for his bed to be made up, and slept soundly until three; some new thought occurring, he then got up to make a few brief notes. From a quarter past three to seven next morning, he slept as peacefully as ever [56].

CHAPTER SIX

And some years ago went to Archangel

JOURNALISTS had been busy from the first instant of the tragedy, preparing accounts to be offered to an intensely curious public at the earliest possible moment. Before these could be produced in the form of books and pamphlets on sale at booksellers everywhere, the columns of journals all over England printed everything they could gather about the assassin, the event, the victim, and everyone associated with the leading characters. From scurrying around to people who had known Bellingham, and from his own comments to jailers and visitors in Newgate, the journalists were able to piece together, though with many distortions, the superficial story of his life. The reality, up to the moment of the assassination, was more complex and more tragic.

Though the public prints insisted unequivocally that the assassin had been born at St Neots (except a few which merely said unhelpfully that he had not), the name of Bellingham does not appear on the parchment pages of the baptism, marriage and burial registers of the fourteenth-century parish church of St Mary the Virgin, St Neots. A brief biography published in 1812 by the Reverend Daniel Wilson, minister of St John's Chapel, Bedford Row, who visited Bellingham the night before his execution, places his birth 'in London about 1771' [57].

His father, another John, is variously described as a land-surveyor and a painter of miniatures; probably the miniature-painter Bellingham who exhibited 'A miniature of a lady' in 1766, and 'Portrait of a gentleman; in miniature' in 1767, at the annual Exhibition of the Society of Artists of Great Britain at the Great Room in Spring Garden. No earlier information about John Bellingham Senior has been traced; but his marriage, while a parishioner of St Martin-in-the-Fields, to Elizabeth Scarbrow, in her parish church of St Dunstan-in-the-West, Fleet Street, is recorded on 12 May 1767 [58].

Elizabeth, who is said to have borne two children to her husband – a first child Mary, who became 'a dressmaker, and a well-disposed young woman, [and] died unmarried', and our John – was herself the daughter of a St Neots family of some standing; her father, William Scarbrow, had progressed through the years in parish records from maltster to yeoman to gentleman. Contemporary accounts suggest that the Bellingham children may have been born in London, after which, Bellingham Senior moved his family to St Neots, where he bought a house and lived for the next five or six years. No records of this transaction remain in the archives of Huntingdonshire. Certainly young John had early associations with St Neots, particularly with his cousin Ann, born in 1767, the daughter of his uncle, Stephen Scarbrow. Ann, obviously fond of her cousin, would be a concerned witness at his trial.

If the young John's infant years were spent happily in the quiet market town of St Neots (even forty years later its population was under two thousand) – scrambling with his cousin in rabbit-populated meadows under pollard willows along the banks of the gently flowing Ouse river, and haunting the town square busily occupied on market days with trade in corn, wine, iron and timber – he had a more troubled boyhood. Around 1779 his father moved back to London and became steadily less competent to care for his small family.

The Bellinghams lived in No. 8, Great Titchfield Street, in a house lately vacated by the diplomatist and writer Caleb Whitefoord (one wonders whether the senior Bellingham may have been acquainted with Whitefoord, or even a protégé, in view of Whitefoord's well-known encouragement of young artists). Here, a block away from the Oxford Market, the little boy grew up in the excitement and bustle of London streets. He probably attended a London school; his petitions and the defence he presented at his trial carried the marks of a good education.

In or around 1780, having shown signs of mental derangement, father Bellingham was committed to St Luke's Hospital (so contemporary reports say, though this is not confirmed by the records in the archives of St Luke's); whence, after a year, he was returned home as incurable, and died shortly afterwards.

Elizabeth Bellingham, if wisdom after the event can be believed, had married her husband against family opposition, and was left with only a small income of under fifty-six pounds a year, but the Scarbrows were clannish, and took an interest in their less fortunate sister. Brother Stephen Scarbrow, who died in September 1781, lay buried in the north chapel of the church where he had been a warden; but sister Mary had made a good marriage, on 20 June 1777 in St George's, Hanover Square, to William Daw, a barrister and Clerk of the King's Silver in the Court of Common Pleas [59].

Uncle Daw, who would remain childless (he had been fifty when he married forty-eight-year-old Mary Scarbrow) henceforth did his best for the fatherless children – rather thanklessly, if the Reverend Daniel Wilson's account of young John is true:

> An obstinate self-will, when removed from his mother's immediate care, is the next step in his career of iniquity. I find that, at the age of fourteen, he was placed as an apprentice with a Mr Love, a jeweller, a man of excellent character, in Whitechapel. Here he was first very perverse and troublesome; and at last ran away from his master, and went to sea in the Hartwell Indiaman; thus betraying, in his boyish years, that dreadful obstinacy of mind which hurried him on at last to the foulest of all crimes [60].

He may have been a troublesome child, now fatherless and probably suffering from the effects of poverty, though every misdemeanour in the earlier life of a villain is apt to be interpreted in the light of his ultimate villainy; nor were people in those days inclined to be tolerant of childish or adolescent naughtiness, a very sign of the devil. At any rate, a goldsmith and hardwareman named James Love did pursue his business at No. 23, Aldgate

High Street at least from 1783 until his death in 1794. As Mr Love was neither a Freeman of the City of London nor a member of the Goldsmiths' Guild, no list of apprentices has survived; nor have any advertisements for John Bellingham as a runaway apprentice been discovered [61].

Uncle Daw's responsibility to the young John did not, however, cease after this escapade, if in fact it was any more serious than a restless dislike of the trade he had been placed in. In 1787, when John would have been around sixteen, Uncle Daw outfitted him as a midshipman or subaltern, so the stories go, and sent him off to sea on the East Indiaman *Hartwell*, a fine new ship of upwards of nine hundred tons, which sailed for China from Gravesend on 21 April 1787, on her maiden voyage, with the prospect of adventure that may have appealed to the boy [62].

Less than a month out from England, genuine adventure overtook young Bellingham, if he was indeed on board [63]. At Gravesend on 20 April, after *Hartwell*'s Captain Edward Fiott had 'rec'd ... sixty Chests of The Honble Comp^y Treasury and three of the Owners and mine with several packages of Private Trade ...' the ship cleared for sea. On 1 May she was in the Downs; on the 4th 'saw the French Coast, too hazy to see what part'. A hint of forthcoming trouble showed up on 8 May, when a member of the crew had to be dismissed as gunner's mate for stealing liquor from the gun room. On 20 May, an officer of the watch discovered an illegal light in the seamen's quarters at night; several of the crew became violently abusive when reprimanded, and had to be placed in irons. Knives were drawn at a subsequent confrontation, and 'a Round Robbin' letter signed by fifty of the crew presented the captain with an ultimatum if the mutineers were to be punished. Two were released, but the ringleader received a dozen lashes.

The trouble grew worse. On the 22nd, 'on my and some of the officers coming on Deck [wrote Fiott in the log] found great part of the crew in the forecastle very tumultious [*sic*] & noisily singing very daring songs and defying all orders from the Officers; in this situation they remained the greatest part of the night.' Armed and ready for any emergency, the officers waited until daylight to take control, when each of the principal ringleaders received two dozen lashes, and it was decided to land nine of the mutineers at the first suitable place. The ship's course was therefore directed to

St Iago [Sao Tiago] in the Cape Verde group 'as the most proper, that Island being inhabited and known to have a Governor'.

Hartwell's log stops abruptly at the end of Wednesday, 23 May. 'Being about three leagues to the N.E. of Bona Vista, one of the Cape de Verd Islands,' reported *The Times* on 13 August when news of disaster arrived, '[*Hartwell*] ran foul of a reef of rocks, and shortly after filled with water.' She sank with a cargo that included jewels and eighty thousand pounds' worth of dollars for the China market.

The subsequent inquiry recommended the dismissal of Captain Fiott and his chief mate, and suspension of the second officer.

It appears that from the time of the Hartwell making the Island of Sal to the hour of the loss of the ship there were such strong instances of the want of ability, prudence and caution both in Captain Fiott and Mr Christie his chief mate, the committee are under the disagreeable necessity of offering as their unanimous opinion that they are unfit to be henceforward employed.

The Times had been puzzled by a wreck that could occur when the mutineers were in irons, the officers properly around, the ship in good condition, with all her studding sails bent for fair weather. No explanation was published.

The Reverend Daniel Wilson dramatized young John's survival: 'He . . . escaped, with only one more, in an open boat.' In fact, all the crew, with the captain, struggled safely ashore. From Bona Vista, Fiott and the purser took passage for England in a Portuguese ship. The chief mate, with twenty-three of the men, fitted the longboat, and for a reason that remains unclear, made a hazardous journey to St Vincent's in the West Indies, when the *William* brought them back to England. The rest of the crew were stranded on barren, sparsely populated Bona Vista until a ship hired by the East India Company arrived to bring them home.

'What makes the loss of this ship more unfortunate and heavy to the India Company, is, that she was richly laden with dollars for the China market, the want of which will be most severely felt by some of the ships that sailed early this season for China, and depended on remittances by this ship, for their homeward bound cargoes,' lamented *The Times*.

No muster list of the ship survives, and Bellingham's name does not appear among the officers or the mutineers, or in the list published later of those midshipmen left at Bona Vista. If he was in fact on board *Hartwell*, he played an insignificant and anonymous part, but one that for a sixteen-year-old boy would be a never-to-be-forgotten adventure. It is an interesting footnote to read that divers managed to rescue much of *Hartwell*'s cargo, including two chests of silver dollars.

The adventure, if young John was part of it, did not impress him with a love of the sea strong enough to return to it. The next date of significance reported in his life was 1794, when a John Bellingham operated a Block Tin Manufactory at No. 97, Oxford Street. 'On his return to England', wrote Wilson, 'he lived an unsettled, and in some instances unprincipled, life till about the year 1793, when he persuaded his excellent mother, from the remnant of her fortune, which he had chiefly exhausted, to establish him in a shop, as a tradesman, in Oxford Street.' Another source assigns his financial backing to long-suffering Uncle Daw, who, 'after much entreaty . . . was induced to advance a pretty large sum, which enabled [Bellingham] to take the shop of a tin-plate worker in Oxford Street' [64].

Not very successfully, it appears. In March 1794, this John Bellingham became bankrupt, and (according to the Reverend Mr Wilson) 'was believed, though it was never legally proved, to have set fire to his own house'. There is, however, little contemporary evidence that Bellingham the bankrupt was Bellingham the assassin; another source – an account written in 1853 that mixes accurate with inaccurate details – is definitely wrong in stating that 'his creditors were not sufficiently satisfied with either his report of the fire, or his conduct, to grant him a certificate; nor did he ever obtain one under this commission.' Creditors of this John Bellingham received dividends in 1795 and 1796, and he was granted a certificate of discharge in March 1799 [65].

Sometime following 1794, says his 1853 chronicler, '[Bellingham] was received into a merchant's counting-house, where he formed connexions; and his employers were induced to commission him beyond seas.' Contemporary journals support this statement, though the quick biographies whipped together by journalists are all equally imprecise about the exact sequence of Bellingham's activities. 'He was brought up in a counting-house in London;

and some years ago went to Archangel...' repeated verbatim in most of the public prints is the nearest anyone got to accounting for this period in his life. It seems difficult to believe that a responsible commercial concern would send an undischarged bankrupt (who had proved his incompetence by his bankruptcy) to represent its interests, involving money transactions, in a foreign country.

His sojourn as a representative in Archangel might, of course, have been during the years following the certificate of discharge (1800–4); but these are years in which other activities have been attributed to him, especially an incident said to have occurred in Hull.

The sequence of events in his life from the wreck in 1787 to his final voyage to Archangel in 1804 is thus confused and full of gaps. It seems likely – if the bankrupt John Bellingham and the assassin were the same person – that he spent these years in gaining experience in the business world: first as an unsuccessful independent businessman, then as a clerk in a London counting-house, then as a representative of a London commercial house living with a Russian merchant in Archangel, and finally operating on his own as a merchant-broker in Liverpool, acting as agent for importers and exporters in the Russian trade, with some business in the Irish trade, and possibly arranging for the insurance of shipping with London insurance companies. A chronology of his life from 1794, therefore, might be said to include a few years in London as an employee, a few more in Archangel as representative, and three or four years as an independent operator in Liverpool prior to his last departure from that city in 1804.

It seems probable that Bellingham would have made frequent visits to most of the mercantile centres in England and Ireland to arrange contracts with local merchants. His 1812 biographers have reported his involvement in a disreputable incident at Hull some time during these years.

> Having formed a connection with a Mr Dorbecker, in the timber line, about ten years ago [1802?] he returned to England in order to seek a contract for the supply of timber; and entered into engagements with the merchants of Hull, for the delivery of deals to the amount of £12,000. Ships were in consequence sent out to Archangel to bring home cargoes; but Mr Dorbecker having meanwhile become a bankrupt,

produce to the value of only between 3 and £4000 was obtained. At this time he behaved in a most unprincipled manner on one or two occasions. Bellingham, who still remained at Hull, was arrested, and thrown into prison, by the disappointed merchants, for the non-fulfilment of the contract; and during his confinement, or soon afterwards, he wrote a pamphlet with the intent of ridiculing the merchants of Hull [66].

The difficult conditions of trade with Russia at the turn of the century, when an embargo had been slapped down in November 1800 by Paul I on all British ships and goods, had been dissipated by the Emperor's assassination in March 1801. The several months of effective disruption nonetheless gave rise to a flurry of court cases in England to settle claims against owners and agents for undelivered cargoes and damaged ships, and agitated meetings were held at Lloyd's Coffee-House to discuss 'some plan for liquidating the claims of the merchants whose vessels have been seized in the Russian ports' [67].

If it is true that Bellingham was in trouble with Hull merchants, it might have been at this time that he was caught in a squeeze. In the light of his vehement denials of guilt in Russia during imprisonment there from 1804 to 1809, the truth or falsity of the Hull episode becomes important: for if he had been guilty of fraud or deception in the past, these later denials must be suspect.

But there are grounds for doubting (or at least wondering about) the truth of this story circulated in 1812. Issues of the *Hull Advertiser* from 1800 to 1805 contain no reports of any case against a Mr Bellingham, or of his subsequent imprisonment in that city: and in 1812, reporting the assassination, the paper repeated the London accounts with little addition or embellishment, simply recording the discrepancy between the bills accepted and the produce delivered, but again making no reference to imprisonment. One pamphlet published by a Hull journalist merely advertised, 'N.B. The Prisoner was well known in Hull about the year 1804' [68].

No record has been traced, in Hull or elsewhere, of the trial or imprisonment of any person named Bellingham, which is surprising, if it happened. Such a loss – for amounts as large as eight or nine thousand pounds – is not usually borne without loud and

public protest. The case would surely have been prosecuted in a
Court higher than that of the Quarter Sessions, where it is not
recorded, and would certainly have got into the public prints,
especially in Hull. Moreover, the *Hull Advertiser*, a chatty and
informal newspaper recording with gusto every item likely to
interest its readers, from accounts of people falling into the harbour and local burglaries netting twelve shillings and the family
linen, to accounts of King's Bench and Assize Court cases all across
the country, makes never a mention of the trial – surely of intense
concern to Hull residents – of anyone remotely likely to be our
John in any issue from 1800 to 1805. Except one: on Saturday,
19 May 1804 (which could have been only a few weeks before
Bellingham sailed from Liverpool on that last fateful voyage), its
columns carried the following statement: 'The debtors of Hull gaol
return thanks to Mr Billingham, of Archangel, for his kind donation of one guinea.'

CHAPTER SEVEN

Extremely ill used and illegally detained

BELLINGHAM'S transactions with Irish merchants and his acquaintance with one John Neville, ship's broker, merchant and auctioneer of Newry, may have introduced him to John's daughter Mary, whom he married around 1803. John Neville, of whose judgement his brother James held no high opinion (James was a merchant in Wigan), was apparently as unsuccessful in business as Bellingham is reported to have been. As a ship's broker he was declared bankrupt in 1797; again bankrupt in 1804, his house and furnishings were sold, and he left Newry for Dublin. Mary – both she and her uncle James consistently spelt their name as Nevill – may have met her husband in Ireland, or in England in the home of relatives. At any rate, it was with Mary, still under twenty, and a baby son, that Bellingham sailed for Archangel from Liverpool in the summer of 1804, in a ship he had personally chartered for what would turn out to be his final trip [69].

Archangel, on the banks of the Dvina River, which falls into the White Sea, was a flat, dreary town in 1804, open to shipping only during midsummer months, and, from its largely wooden construction, subject to disastrous fires. It was, however, Russia's principal northern commercial port, and indeed was the most important port in Russia until St Petersburg (now Leningrad) was built in

1702. A community of British merchants was established in Archangel as early as the 1550s, becoming an organized body known as the British Factory, in 1716, 'the factors having united for the purpose of regulating the charges on goods and ships, chiefly in order to raise the necessary funds for their church establishment'. In 1802, exports from the area were valued at just over five million roubles, and Britain was the oldest and biggest customer, taking at that time about eighty-five per cent of the timber, tallow and iron. In 1803, the number of English ships arriving in Russian ports was more than half the total of all foreign ships [70].

For what happened in Archangel and subsequently in St Petersburg we have only Bellingham's side of the story, except for the statements of Lord Granville Leveson Gower, the British Ambassador, and Sir Stephen Shairp, the Consul-General, who accepted the word of the Russian authorities without, it seems, much investigation into the case. They were, of course, hardly in a position to accuse the Russian officials of lying unless they were prepared to dig more deeply into the rights and wrongs at issue.

From the beginning, Bellingham protested his innocence, and maintained that innocence vigorously and consistently throughout the years that followed. 'He was there very troublesome to the government, sending to them memorial after memorial, on subjects relative to his private concerns,' was the way his impassioned protests were described in 1812 by British journalists, when the horror of his incredible solution to the problem was darkening every action in his past. Memorial after memorial he did indeed send to the officials; but whether these were the evasions of an incompetent businessman compelled to save face by denial of truth, or – as he insisted – the writhings of an innocent victim caught in the toils of injustice, it is probably impossible to judge at this distance of time. If he were indeed a victim of devious Russian contrivance, imagination must recoil from too close a study of the bitter years he had to dwell on his situation.

'He was one of those unhappy men who are driven to a state of insanity by not being able to bear misfortunes, and especially misfortunes proceeding from what they deem wrongs,' wrote William Cobbett, who was imprisoned in Newgate in 1812 for libel, and witnessed Bellingham's execution [71].

The ultimate solution he chose for the redress he had sought in vain in Russia and in England bears enough marks of insanity to make the arguments meaningless, whatever they may have been in fact. 'I am one', he might have said with the Second Murderer, '. . . whom the vile blows and buffets of the world / Have so incens'd that I am reckless what / I do to spite the world' [72].

The trouble seems to have arisen when a Russian-owned ship, *Sojus [Soyuz]*, under a captain Milreay, was lost in the White Sea in the autumn of 1803 [73]. An attempt by the owners 'to obtain an irregular Insurance out of Lloyd's Coffee-House' was apparently circumvented by an anonymous letter giving the true story of her loss, in which some fraud was involved. Bellingham was suspected as the writer of the letter by Soloman Van Brienen, one of two brothers operating the eighty-year-old House of R. Van Brienen, Sons, who, with Vassiley Popoff, member of a well-known and wealthy merchant family in Archangel, were owners of the ship. Vassiley Popoff happened at the time also to be mayor of the city [74].

'Had the supposition . . . proved true,' Bellingham insisted, 'this masked detention was intended to be dropped, and ⌊I⌋ was to have been prosecuted for the amount of the Insurance on the Sojus, which the Underwriters at Lloyd's refused to pay.' The accusation having been proved false, and the owners thus discomfited and out of pocket, they were forced to reimburse their loss by other means; having a scapegoat handy, they proceeded to accuse Bellingham of a debt of 4,890 roubles (the current exchange rate was about ten roubles to the pound) owed to a Mr Conrad Dorbecker, a bankrupt for whom Van Brienen and his colleagues were assignees.

Having been quite unconscious of such indebtedness (as he would maintain throughout), Bellingham made his preparations to return home via St Petersburg, as the winter had by now closed the port of Archangel. Russian travel regulations at that time were exceedingly strict, and remarked on by most of the adventurous visitors who recorded their impressions of a land still romantic and mysterious to English readers.

The cautionary rules, in regard to travellers quitting the town, are . . . strict [commented Henry Storch, whose account appeared in 1801]. These must publish in the newspaper their name, their quality, and their place of abode, three several

times, and produce the news-papers containing the advertisement, as a testimonial, in the government from which they then
receive their passport, without which it is next to impossible
to get out of the empire. This regulation not only secures the
creditor of the person about to depart, but also enables the
police to keep a closer inspection over all suspected inhabitants [75].

Accordingly, Bellingham had equipped himself with the required travelling pass for St Petersburg on 15 November 1804,
and was on the point of leaving when the pass was suddenly
recalled. For the next three months, while not actually imprisoned,
he was harassed by restriction on his movements and continued
supervision by both military and civil officers, and also under frequent call to appear before Governor-General Furster with the
assignees of the bankrupt Dorbecker while the claims against him
were sorted out.

On 1 June 1807 in St Petersburg, three years after his first arrest
in Archangel, and still confined, Bellingham produced a concise
account of what had happened. He called in the Reverend Benjamin Beresford, who was acting as officiating minister of the
British congregation in the Russian capital, and made a sworn
statement, certified by Alexander Shairp on behalf of his brother
Sir Stephen, British Consul-General in Russia, 'in witness whereof
I have hereunto set my hand & the Seal of my Arms'. Distraught
as he was by this time, Bellingham's careful, even handwriting
bears no sign of the turmoil then seething in his heart.

I John Bellingham British subject and Mercht of Liverpool
at present under arrest in the College of Commerce St Petersburg, finding my health considerably deranged by an illegal
detention in prison in justice to myself and Family have
thought it prudent for many reasons to make the following
solemn declaration upon oath –
That I arrived at Archangel from Liverpool in a vessel chartered by myself for mercantile purposes in the summer of
1804, and was illegally prevented from returning to England
by the said ship as was my intention, and also was so much
injured as to be deprived of the opportunity of loading my
own goods on board of her and for which she was expressly

chartered, which detention and prevention occasioned me very serious losses.

On the 16th [*sic*] Novr following I took out a travelling pass or petrovnick for St Petersburg and on the evening of the same day, the said petrovnick was forcibly taken from me by the police Master without any cause whatever, and soldiers and police officers were placed on [my] person day and night to prevent [my] quitting the place . . .

He did not bear these trials silently. Through January and February 1805 his letters of protest reached the Governor-General almost daily. The original claim against him, he said, had been for 38,000 roubles (£3,800), perhaps the amount the claimants had hoped to recover to replace the insurance they had failed to get.

It was a sum 'which progressively dwindled to nothing', Bellingham would write in another petition nearly a year later. By the end of January the claim had been reduced to 4,890 roubles, but Bellingham denied owing even this sum. On the 23rd, and again on 8 February, he clamoured once more for release of his pass 'and furnishing a petrovnick for me and my Servant to St Petersburg'. His young wife, already arrived and waiting for him in that city, seems to have been allowed to travel ahead of him.

To his request, it seems the Governor-General acceded: evidence had been brought clearing Bellingham of indebtedness. In the early stages of the dispute, a Mr Christian Grell had been called in by the assignees to examine the books of both parties, and 'In consequence he reported to them that it appeared Mr Dorbecker had used [me] extremely ill, and . . . thought it equitable for both parties to relinquish claims, which some time after took place, and Mr Grell was advised of . . .'

Probably as a result of this decision, Bellingham got his pass back, though not for long. Having got it, he made his preparations to set off on the long-deferred journey. But on 3 March, just as he was passing the borders of the province, he was seized, hauled from his *kabitky* or travelling sledge, and brought back to appear before the Duma (municipal council), where he found that Mr Van Brienen, having persuaded the complaisant Governor-General to reverse his verdict, had had him declared a prisoner.

'In consequence of the account having been settled to your

perfect satisfaction,' wrote Bellingham indignantly on 12 May, after a good deal of turbulent water had passed under the bridge, 'you returned my pass, and I went with the police Master to Mr Solomon van Brienen by your order on another trifling business – who introduced fresh matters to the police Master and denied to him all that had passed before you.'

On 5 March, two days after the ignominious capture at the border, he was committed to the *Hauptwacht* (guardhouse). The appalled prisoner wrote on the 4th, while still in the Duma:

> Am persuaded it is impossible for your Excellency to be apprised of this circumstance, otherwise am sure you send an immediate order for my liberation.
>
> As expressly declared before your Excellency by the Assignees through their Bevolmachtiger [deputy] Mr Soloman Brienen they had given into & were agreed in every point with but a single exception, which was for a parcel of Iron [in the sum of r4,890] – and at same time as is well known to you, they declined giving any account in writing although I requested it. I have confuted in their own handwriting having any thing to do with the Iron which Mr van Brienen afterwards confirmed to the policy [*sic*] Master, consequently I have nothing more to do with the Assignees in any shape. So the affair hangs, and the matter remains with you and the policy Master to determine wether [*sic*] I am indebted or not. As you must be clearly convinced I am not indebted to them, I both hope and expect an immediate order for my liberation after this notice, or request the favor of your reason in writing why you suffer my detention.

Worse was to come.

> The Domé [Duma] took possession of his Portmanteau [wrote Bellingham] and ordered it to be sealed for the purpose of forcibly possessing themselves of his Books, private Letters, accounts and documents in express violation of the 18th Article of the Treaty of Commerce, nor did he get repossession of said portmanteau till after having petitioned for the purpose and was obligated to expose the contents in the most public manner displaying every article of wearing apparel

separately to demonstrate there not being any Book, Letter, paper or document of any kind.

Beyond this humiliation, heavier guns were brought to bear. During the hearing at which Van Brienen introduced new claims, Bellingham, with increasing disbelief, heard the Governor-General repudiate his earlier position. His fury got the better of him and led him into an outburst. When, some time in April, Sir Stephen Shairp, the British Consul, wrote at Bellingham's request for information about the case, Shairp was blandly told that the prisoner's detention was legal and that, moreover, his conduct had been 'highly indecorous'.

He wrote bitterly to the Governor-General on 12 May:

> If on this occasion I acted a little vociferous or as it has been termed highly indecorous, surely it was pardonable as arising from circumstances I thought morally impossible to exist. In a conversation with your Excellency at the time the pass was given to me, you acknowledged that the Assignees had all along acted beyond the Law, and if I thought proper could seek redress. Afterwards, when the Assignees accompanied by three gentlemen came together before you, this conversation was introduced by me – which, however, you were pleased to deny, and before them said quite the contrary, and was astonished I could have the assurance to assert it to your face – as also that the account had been arranged before you, although, wonderful to relate, Mr Brienen and you supported each other in denying it.
>
> These are truths which your own conscience must confirm, and though disacknowledged, yet the facts remain.

He was aware of his presumption in addressing an official in these terms. 'This is a singular and entire new style of writing to a man of your exalted rank. The occasion of it is also equally new and singular, therefore [I] flatter myself that one will palliate the other.'

His protests availed him nothing, and he now found himself deserted, as he felt, by the British authorities. It was this desertion that would fester through all the rest of his life. The Ambassador,

Lord Granville Leveson Gower, wrote on 6 May, in response to Bellingham's several letters and carefully copied correspondence:

> I am sorry to find that you are involved in so unpleasant a dispute at Archangel, but however desirous I may be of assisting you, it is not in my power to forward any Application for permission for you to come to St Petersburgh [sic] on your sole representation of the Circumstances of the Transaction in question, particularly as I find this Statement contradicted by the Letter of the Governor General of Archangel to Mr Shairp.
>
> At the same time, however, that I say this, I wish you to understand, that provided you can furnish me with such Evidence of your having been unjustly used, as will authorize my Interference on this subject, I shall very readily take such steps in your behalf as the occasion may appear to me to require.

If, in fact, Bellingham ever did have any such documentary evidence, it was probably out of his reach by now, after the seizure and public examination of the papers in his portmanteau. For what it is worth as evidence of the truth of his account of the dispute, it should be remembered that his letters setting out his version were written, not later from possibly prejudiced memory, but while he remained in the hands of his accusers.

One small, bright spot appeared on his horizon. The Procureur of Archangel, one Ivan Fedorisch Makcemove, reported to Prince Lapuchin, the Minister of Justice, that Bellingham was 'extremely ill used and illegally detained', and though no action resulted, it helped to improve his morale. After having been imprisoned 'like a felon' for a full six months, he was released early in September, apparently giving some kind of parole to the authorities on the sixth of that month.

On 9 October, still unable to leave Archangel, he penned a lengthy sixteen-section petition to the *Graschdanskaja Palata* (State Court) appealing against the Duma's resolution of 9 March awarding the verdict to the assignees, of which he first heard on 5 October.

> The resolution sets forth by stating that the Domé appointed three persons ... namely Christian Grell, Francis

Cropp and Stephen Morgan in conformity to the 19th Article of the Treaty of Commerce to examine into the differences between the Assignees and petitioner, and no legal objection being made thereto on the part of the petitioner, said three persons found him really indebted the above sum [4,890 roubles]. To which the Petitioner has the following comments and objects to urge –

1st That at the period the Domé pretended to take cognizance of the affair, Petitioner was in no account with the Assignees whatever, everything having been settled some time before by each party mutually withdrawing their pretentions [sic] – save and except for a parcel of Iron for which they demanded the forementioned sum. Petitioner then said, and says now – if the Assignees will furnish him with an account and it is found right he is willing to pay the money. The affair was put into the Police the beginning of February last; when Petitioner applied to the Police Master on the Business [he] was told by him [that] the money must be paid first and the account rendered afterwards.

2ndly – So far to the contrary of making no legal objection, Petitioner made the most legal of all objections, viz. that he had no account whatever to settle – nor had he any difference with the Assignees of any kind except for the Iron, and urged that on proving a good title to their pretentions, he was willing to acknowledge his responsibility and deposit the Money . . .

3 . . . As the Assignees themselves disclaimed along ago having any claim on him for the Iron he is totally ignorant to the present moment on what they ground their pretentions . . .

He was especially disillusioned by what he regarded as the treachery of Christian Grell, 'who evidently is a man of very feeble integrety'. Mr Grell's original decision had been in his favour – 'Yet it appears this same Mr Grell afterwards came forward and put his name to some paper testifying he found [me] truly and lawfully indebted to the Assignee of Mr Dorbecker . . .
In his tenth section, Bellingham engaged 'to prove by the Assignees themselves, as also by the three persons nominated by

the Domé that no account existed at the time, and that each individual knew the whole to be a fiction and fable intended to cover the former henious [sic] conduct of the Assignees, as well as to screen other persons who had aided and assisted in their diabolical irregularities . . .' If he were allowed to examine the representatives of both sides on oath, such interrogation 'would sett the real circumstances in their proper light'.

Needless to say, he was allowed no such privilege.

On 11 October, his petition completed but as yet not sealed for delivery, Bellingham received a further resolution from the Duma: '. . . wherein is declared they made known to him . . . their resolution on the same day and that he then nor since made any objection thereto, and consequently forfeited the right of appellation'.

He penned an outraged postscript to what he had just finished writing:

> Whereas Petitioner never so much as heard of said resolution till copy thereof was delivered to him on the 5th Inst; so much to the contrary, the suit has been going on ever since, and Petitioner has been perpetually complaining [he had indeed] which is a complete refutation of the assertion. Moreover, Petitioner declares he never was called from the Hauptwacht to the Domé but once, and that for the purpose of opening and exposing the contents of his portmanteau . . .

A new civil governor, Baron Asch, who had come to Archangel around this time, gave Bellingham some hope.

> To him I stated the cruel circumstances under which I was detained. He very candidly said that I was either innocent or guilty: if innocent I ought to be discharged, and if guilty I ought to be tried. He took up my cause, for I had no friends besides: I was surrounded by enemies; but he generously stepped forward, and bringing the matter into a Court of Justice, I obtained judgment against the whole party, including the Military Governor who had injured me.

Whatever the reason, Bellingham's travel pass was now suddenly returned to him, properly endorsed, and he made arrangements to leave Archangel forthwith, after notifying the police on 18 October with the following statement.

The Assignees of Mr Dorbecker not having established their claim as required by Law after a complete investigation of the affair in the Dooma – the obligation I gave on the 6th Sepr is entirely done away – and moreover the Procureur has reported that I have been illegally detained. Therefore this is to give notice that I purpose parting for St Petersburg in a few days unless legal cause is shewn to the contrary in writing, notice of which have also been given to His Excellency the General Governor & Procureur.

CHAPTER EIGHT

Bandied from prison to prison

THIS time, no one stopped him, no one hauled him back in humiliating custody from the provincial border. He reached St Petersburg early in November 1805, and one can imagine his happy reunion with Mary Ann, and with his small son.

St Petersburg at that time was the wonder of foreign beholders. 'This marvellous city' on the banks of the wide blue Neva river had almost overwhelmed Sir John Carr a few years earlier, with its

> glorious river, adorned with stupendous embankments of granite . . . its sides lined with palaces, stately buildings, and gardens . . . green cupolas, and the lofty spires of the Greek churches covered with ducat gold, and glittering in the sun . . . the magnificent railing of the summer gardens, with its columns and vases of granite, a matchless work of imperial taste and splendour [76].

In this city of spacious streets, crowded with carriages and rich equipages drawn by four horses, magnificent houses, elegant churches, and with immense numbers of shops and stores, Bellingham remained free for some months, though under the necessity required of all foreigners to make his residence known to the police, and still deprived of his passport. If he had kept quiet and cut his losses, it is possible he might have been allowed to leave

Russia at this point. But (as someone in Hull would recall in 1812) though he was 'perfectly cool and collected, [and] very difficult to irritate', he could be 'violent and implacable in his enmity, when his passions were excited' [77]. His gadfly dignity would not let him rest: he promptly impeached His Excellency the Governor-General to the Imperial Senate 'for having publicly sanctioned an improper oath knowing it to be so', for having lied to British consular officials, and for the illegal detention he had suffered. He also demanded remuneration for the losses incurred while he had been prevented from transacting business.

A bravo, a foolish, and – if guilty – a dangerous move. Did Mary Ann, with her solid commonsense, argue against this futile urge to even the score, as she had to do years later?

At a time when Englishmen were generally in disfavour in the current Napoleonic climate of changing political and military alignments, the result might have been expected. Only five years earlier, Edward Daniel Clarke, traveller and writer, had been distressed by the treatment of his countrymen in Russia, 'and particularly in St Petersburg [where] they were constantly liable to be interrupted in the streets and public places [by the police] and treated with impertinence'. Only two years later, the Treaty of Tilsit would sever British diplomatic relations with Russia. It was, apart from the merits of Bellingham's case, a bad time for an English merchant of no significance to challenge the might and authority of Russian law [78].

On 5 June, a Senate ukase ordered Bellingham arrested on both criminal and civil charges: for 'having quitted Archangel in a clandestine manner', and for a debt of 'two thousand roobles to some persons at Archangel', so Bellingham described the accusations. Mysteriously, the 4,890 roubles at issue up to now had in some manner melted away to less than half, and Bellingham insisted all through that he was never able to find out, in this new charge, 'the name of the Plaintiff or the nature of the debt'.

He was arrested on 11 June, and held first in the *Hoffgerichte* (the high court of justice) and then in the *Thurm* (town prison), while inquiries were made at Archangel to verify his claim that he did indeed hold a properly endorsed pass. Its validity was ascertained forty days later, and the criminal charge was dismissed; but 'to my great surprise I was committed to the Thurm on the 20th July for the forementioned pretended debt of 2000 roobles'. When on 27 August he appeared before the High Criminal Court to explain his non-payment, Bellingham replied: 'Because I do not owe it, but if I do owe it, it is all the same to me to whom the money is paid – therefore if the Palata will have the goodness to produce a proper document on which it is demanded I would settle that instant.'

His reply was apparently regarded as impertinence. Back he went to the Thurm for three days on bread and water.

Prison conditions in Russia even a dozen years later have been described as barbaric. 'The dreadful picture of men and women, young and old, guilty and innocent, crowded together in dark, damp, underground quarters without beds, ventilation, or adequate food had scarcely changed since the days of John Howard' (who visited the prisons of St Petersburg in the 1780s). Stephen Grellet (Etienne de Grellet du Mabillier) was writing with disgust at the end of 1818 about the 'great filthiness [that] prevails in many of these places. Various kinds of vermin are numerous. The bed-bugs are seen in clusters on the walls, like swarms of bees on the sides of their hives. The air is noxious ... so impure that it much affected our heads and our stomachs.' Early in 1819 he remarked that the prisons 'do not appear to have been cleaned for years' [79].

During the seventy-two days of confinement suffered by Bellingham after his arrest in June 1806, he was 'bandied from prison to prison, and from dungeon to dungeon, fed on bread and water, treated with the utmost cruelty, and frequently marched through the streets under a military guard with felons and criminals of the most atrocious description, even before the residence of the British Minister, who might view from his window, this degrading severity towards a British subject...' Eventually, on 1 October, he was transferred to the custody of the College of Commerce, 'a tribunal established for the special purpose of taking cognizance of commercial matters relating to British subjects, and whose authority was recognized in the commercial treaty between the two countries' [80]. Here he would remain for the next two and a half years, the first three months in close confinement. For a man of Bellingham's fastidious temperament, the conditions of his imprisonment would have been hard to bear.

His torment was increased by worry about Mary Ann (once more pregnant) and his little son, stranded and unprotected in this strange city. It is not clear just when she left St Petersburg; she was eventually rescued by the kindness of unnamed English gentlemen, and made the long journey home in the eighth month of her pregnancy. The reassuring news that she had found refuge with her kindly Quaker uncle, James Nevill, a 'heel-maker' in Wigan, Lancashire, and that a second son had been born, probably never reached Bellingham [81].

From the beginning of 1807, he was allowed out into the streets from time to time, but only to go out 'like a prisoner under serious criminal arrest', accompanied by a guard. On some of these forays he tried once again to enlist British aid, seeking asylum in the Embassy. Lord Gower had been appointed to a second term in April 1807, though he took his time about getting to Russia, and did not arrive until the end of June.('I know . . . that it was material to Lord G. L. Gower to get over his election before he left England,' wrote Francis James Jackson, envoy to Denmark, to his brother Sir George, 'and perhaps it may be thought that such great personages could not move without having taken due time for preparation. But should one moment have been lost, beyond the time necessary for recognizing and digesting their instructions?' [82])

At the end of July, according to Lord Gower, Bellingham 'came running into my house one evening, and solicited me to allow him to remain all night, in order to avoid being retaken into custody by the police, from whom he had escaped. I complied with the request, though I could not, upon any ground, assume to myself the power of protecting him from legal arrest' [83]. On 30 July, he penned a note to Bellingham, who was still within the Embassy:

> I cannot think myself justified under the circumstances of your case in exerting the privilege of the House of the Ambassador to protect you from the custody of the Police Officer who escorted you here. I must therefore request you to give yourself up again into his custody, but shall think it my Duty to make representations to the Government upon your affair, & shall be happy to use any means in my Power towards forwarding an arrangement of the Business in which you are involved [84].

Russia's severance of relations with Britain in the following

November cut off further hope (if he still had had hope) of any support Bellingham could have expected from the Ambassador. In 1812, Lord Gower would state, however, that he remembered 'in conversation with the minister for foreign affairs, expressing my personal wish that the Russian government, seeing no prospect of recovering the sum of money required from him, would liberate him from prison, on condition of his immediately returning to England' [85].

No such luck. In July 1807 the Senate, with the College of Commerce, had instituted preliminary steps to have Bellingham declared a bankrupt. 'On account of the non-payment of this sum [the 2,000 roubles alleged now to be owing to Dorbecker's estate] Mr Bellingham is detained in the said College and has there declared that he has neither money nor effects with him here, his whole property being in England.' Until the assignees in Archangel could be informed, and take the proper legal steps, 'Bellingham is to be kept under inspection of the Executor and then to be . . . kept in the City Prison' [86].

He would have caustic comment on these statements. He denied emphatically that he had ever said he was unable to pay because all his property was in England. And he continued to refuse a demand to pay the two thousand roubles 'or even twenty rubles', as a token payment that would acknowledge the justice of the demand. He was actually afraid to do so.

> I was aware if I had done this, I should justify the conduct of the Senate, and the military Governor of Archangel, against whom I had obtained a legal decision, with an acknowledgement that I had been unjustly treated. The necessary consequence would be, that for my supposed contumacy in bringing a false charge against the Senate and the Governor, I should be sent to Siberia [87].

In October 1809, without warning, he seems to have been released from close confinement, and 'forcibly expelled from the College without a pass, to take refuge where he would'. This was a serious matter: the Russian system of security, apart from the stringent travel regulations, made life difficult for persons without fixed address. 'Every householder and innkeeper is obliged to declare to the police who lodges with him, or what strangers have put up at his house,' wrote Storch in 1801. 'If a stranger or lodger stays out all night, the landlord must inform the police of it at latest on the third day of his absence from his house' [88]. Bellingham, however, highly suspect and without a necessary travel pass, would have remained under the supervision of the authorities in any case. In mid-December, the unfortunate man took the somewhat desperate step of sending a petition to the Czar himself. A contemporary copy of the document, with impressively notarized translation, is still extant.

> To His Most Imperial Majesty Alexander Pavlovitch, emperator and autocrator of all the Russias &c &c &c. Petition of John Bellingham, brittish subject as follows:

> The petitioner has been detained in the Empire of Russia near five years – the last two years and half, he has been under criminal and civil arrest in St Petersburg, the former being done away the College of Commerce proceeded to final judgment on the charge on the 3d June last (1808) and in consequence thereof refered [sic] to the Liquidation Commission to bring the affair to a final arrangement, and furnish the necessary clearance that he might obtain his pass for his Departure, but notwithstanding this referance [sic] and his repeated solicitations so to do, the said commission positively refuses to espouse his cause.

> Therefore he most humbly implores your Imperial Majesty will most graciously order said commission to furnish him with the necessary clearance and [to the end, he remained consistent in his demands for redress] at the same time remunerate him for the loss of time occasioned to his prejudice by such long detention ...

In 1812 the *Liverpool Mercury* recounted his daring in petitioning the Emperor:

> While he was in prison, Bellingham wrote a long petition, stating his grievances, which he sent direct by post to the Emperor. The postmaster fearful of the consequences, at first refused to receive the letter, but at length, unwillingly agreed to forward it on condition that Bellingham signed a paper

acknowledging himself to be the author of it. Of this petition, however, it did not appear that any notice was taken [89].

Perhaps it is needless to repeat that the appeal was ignored. Ten more months were to pass before any action was taken. But the cat finally grew bored with teasing the mouse. 'At length the Senate, quite tired out by these severities, in 1809 I received, at midnight, a discharge from my confinement, with a pass, and an order to quit the Russian dominions' [90].

He reached his native land early in December 1809, just five years after all the trouble had begun. He brought with him a burning resentment against what he regarded as his abandonment by the British Government, and an iron belief that, now his innocence had been vindicated by the fact of his release, he was entitled to legal redress for his sufferings and his losses.

CHAPTER NINE

My mercantile existence has been totally annihilated

THE first thing Bellingham did when he arrived in England (out of the blue, it must have seemed to astonished relatives and friends) was try to discover where his wife and children were. He wrote to Mary's uncle, James Nevill, in Wigan, and then got in touch with his cousin and childhood playmate, Ann Scarbrow, now the widow of a St Neots gentleman, Edward Billett, and living in London with two young daughters, one born after the death of her father. She may have been the Mrs *Billit* residing at No. 104, *Sloan* Street that year: she was a widow of some means [*91*]. Both Uncle James and Cousin Ann could tell him about Mary, and he wrote to her at once. So did Ann, to tell her the good news. Mary was supporting herself and her two children as a milliner in Liverpool, in partnership with another Mary, Miss Stevens, whom she had met in Wigan through her friendship with this Mary's aunt.

Though he seems to have written constantly to his Mary, Bellingham did not at once go to Liverpool. He was already in the grip of his fatal obsession, and turned immediately to the process of setting the right wheels in motion. He was not without funds. While he was trapped in Russia, Uncle Daw had died, moderately wealthy, in September 1808, aged eighty, at his residence in Hans Place, Knightsbridge; Mary Daw had lived for only a month longer. She died childless at the age of seventy-nine, and her will, proved 27 October 1808 (indicating Ann Billett as executrix) bequeathed a portion of her considerable estate to her sister Elizabeth, John Bellingham's mother. Elizabeth had died some years earlier (in 1802 or 1803, in Liverpool, according to varying accounts, though no record of death or will has been traced). Her share, which now came to her son, was reported by several of the newspapers at the time of Bellingham's notoriety as amounting to four hundred pounds [92].

On 27 December, shortly after his return to England, Bellingham had a petition ready for presentation to the Marquis of Wellesley, then Foreign Secretary, in which he set out his wrongs and his claims in detail. In the meantime, he poured out his plans to sympathetic Ann, who, doubtless having many times before encountered her cousin's interesting flights of fancy, listened with indulgent but sceptical attention. Harmless dreams, she probably thought at first: an escape valve justifiably allowable after his horrid Russian experiences.

He spent Christmas 1809 with Ann in London, talking endlessly about

> his great schemes that he had pursued, he said that he had realized more than an hundred thousand pounds, with which he intended to buy an estate in the west of England, and to take a house in London: I asked him where the money was, he said he had not got the money, but it was the same as if he had, for that he had gained his cause in Russia, and our government must make it good to him [93].

He had taken lodgings at No. 53, Theobalds Road, and here Mary joined him for a brief visit early in 1810 (though she may have stayed with Ann). On 31 January came the first rebuff – a letter from the Foreign Office, signed by Charles Culling Smith, to say 'that his Majesty's government is precluded from interfering in the support of your case, in some measure, by the circumstances of the case itself, and entirely so at the present moment, by the suspension of intercourse with the Court of St Petersburg' [94].

Bellingham could see no reason why suspension of diplomatic relations should affect his claim on the British Government for neglect of support as a British subject. To 'The Right Honorable the Lords Commissioners of His Majesty's Treasury' he fired off another petition on 16 February, repeating his claims and arguing that his 'mercantile existence has been totally annihilated, and he is now with a family involved in ruin'; suspension of intercourse between the two countries was no excuse to deny him redress. A week later he was informed that 'my Lords are not able to afford you any relief' [95].

This door closed, Bellingham next tried the Privy Council, with no better success. 'It is [not] a matter in which their Lordships can, in any manner, interfere.' An approach to Perceval himself, as Chancellor of the Exchequer, fared no better: on 27 May, Perceval's secretary, Thomas Brooksbank, wrote, 'that the time for presenting private petitions has long since passed, and that Mr Perceval cannot encourage you to expect his sanction in introducing into the House a petition, which Mr Perceval thinks is not of a nature for the consideration of Parliament' [96].

Perceval had not been active in politics when Bellingham left England in 1804, but he had been a rising man, a man to watch. In the 1790s, long before his entry into Parliament as a Member for Northampton in 1806, he had earned the good opinion of influential men in the Government by his achievements in courts of law, and by his keen interpretation of constitutional questions. He had received several official appointments before entering political life, and was highly regarded for his uncompromising support for causes he believed in – the war with France, Pitt's stern taxation policies, and the necessity to maintain legal restrictions against Catholics (though he was more liberal in his warm support for abolition of the slave trade).

He had become Solicitor-General in 1801, Attorney-General in 1802. It was his attack on the Catholic policy of the Ministry of All the Talents that helped to defeat that Government, and he was appointed to the post of Chancellor of the Exchequer in Lord Portland's ministry in 1807. Portland's illness in 1809 led to some manoeuvring for position and eventually ended with Perceval's becoming Prime Minister, combining the post with the one he already held in the Exchequer, which had found no takers. His personal integrity (though he seems to have supported continuation of patronage and sinecures in many cases) did not allow him to accept the salary for the latter appointment.

Perhaps the dissensions and disagreements among the strong men of the party – Castlereagh, Canning, Sidmouth, Wellesley – kept the administration weaker than it should have been; or the vigour of opponents like Whitbread, Burdett and Brougham. Moreover, the costly progress of the war and its consequent economic drain on the country increased the Government's unpopularity. The final loss of the King's senses and the Regency crisis in 1811 meant further constitutional struggles, shot through with strong emotional allegiances that further divided the country's leaders. 'He carried on the government single-handed, prosecuted the war, defeated his opponents, and disarmed his critics,' was *The Dictionary of National Biography*'s verdict, but it added: 'A man of strong will and decisive character, he can, however, hardly be credited with possessing either "the information or the genius essential to an English minister at that momentous epoch." '

This was the man, as leader and figurehead of the government, against whom Bellingham finally pitted himself, though he would patiently exhaust all other approaches before he made the last irreversible one.

Six full months of persistent but fruitless hammering at doors had at last convinced both Mary and Cousin Ann that his intentions were serious, and both began to feel concern and apprehension – though this would have been for his own sake: for the ultimate thanklessness of his efforts rather than for any fear of desperate measures. Ann remembered his father's mental confusions, Mary, perhaps, his defiant and disastrous challenge to the mighty in Russia. He was, it seemed from his reiterated plan for redress, off on something of the same crusade.

'Neither she nor I gave any credit to it,' Ann would recall.

Annoyed by their lack of faith, he took them both one day to the Secretary of State's office, where, only because he had ladies with him, a Mr Smith agreed to see him.

' "Sir," said Bellingham, "my friends say that I am out of my senses, is it your opinion, Mr Smith, that I am so?" '

Mr Smith was tactful. ' "It is a very delicate question for me to answer, I only know you upon this business, and I can assure you, that you will never have what you are pursuing after." '

They then withdrew, Ann and Mary both by now embarrassed and indignant at having been made to appear ridiculous. Bellingham, however, seemed complacently assured. Did his obsessed ears hear words quite different from those his wife and Ann had heard? In the coach he patted Mary's hand soothingly. ' "Now I hope, my dear, you are well convinced all will happen well, and as I wished" ' [97].

Very well worth reading would be a diary written by this young woman, who at twenty had made the perilous sea journey to an unknown land, travelled alone (except for a baby son) the five hundred miles from Archangel to St Petersburg, waited in fearful uncertainty for a husband in deep trouble, returned pregnant and unprotected to England, and – even then not more than twenty-six – supported herself and two children for five full years.

Back in Liverpool in 1810 after the reunion with her husband, she pondered the wisdom of resuming the relationship. She decided at first that she 'would not live with him untill he made a Solemn promise to give up wrong thoughts of his wild goose schemes & expectations'. Uncle James Nevill would later rue the advice he gave her: 'I was one that advised her to live with him "as she had taken him for better or for worse".' At the time, the advice seemed sound. Bellingham, despondent over his frustrations, accepted Mary's ultimatum and returned at last to Liverpool to renew his business connections and try to forget the past. 'This he did most solemnly promise & even burnt a parcell of papers which he stated was those belonging to the affair' [98].

He was not, however, a man who could forget. The injustices of the past, as he saw them, cut too deep; they rankled and raged, perhaps the more strongly because this was now a subject taboo in his household, the cause of tight-lipped argument and recriminations. He tried, though. He went about his business in Liverpool with some competence, travelling to Dublin where his father-in-law John Neville was now a merchant, to develop connections for the Irish trade. He set up a warehouse in Park Lane, near the Old Dock, and moved into the home at No. 46, Duke Street with his wife and two little boys and Miss Stevens. Everyone, by now, even business associates, avoided raising the subject of Russia, to head off the inevitable outburst [99].

CHAPTER TEN

Carte blanche, *to act in whatever manner I thought proper*

AFTER this first flurry of petitions and the family arguments that had resulted, Bellingham made no further approach to the Government for about eighteen months. He continued his operations as a ship-broker in Liverpool, contracting for cargoes and arranging insurance, while Mary ran her millinery business from the Duke Street house, in partnership with Mary Stevens, and looked after her little sons. Henry, the baby, was born in the summer of 1811.

Life probably looked better to Mary now than it had for many a day. Her husband was home again after all the years when she had feared she was a widow. He was a kindly man, good to her and the children. The little boys were growing nicely, and if John's commercial undertakings were not always highly profitable (there is no reason to believe he was a commercial failure at this time), her millinery business filled the gap and kept the family from dire need. At least he seemed to have forgotten his peculiar ideas about getting recompense for his losses and his sufferings.

Whether Mary Bellingham's repudiation of her husband's obsessive campaign for redress came from a disillusioned certainty that the Government would not recognize claims, however just, or whether she knew how shifting were the sands on which those claims had been built, cannot now be known. She may have disagreed with him out of a fund of commonsense that saw no use in continuing to batter against unresponsive walls; or perhaps she was, in fact, unhappily aware that on this subject at least his mind had tipped over the edge of sanity, and that not his story but the Russians' was the truth. It seems possible that she half-believed him. She clearly cared for him. While she may have thought him impractical and credulous, it is unlikely that she believed him to be dishonest. She probably thought him silly rather than deranged.

She was living in a fool's paradise. Bellingham may have kept quiet to preserve the family peace, but he could not free his mind from the seething sense of injustice that refused to let him rest, and perhaps it festered the more dangerously because he could not now talk about it. His mind closed around it until he was almost turned in upon himself. It must have been difficult for him to go about his everyday business with any appearance of interest or any effective concentration, when the necessity of obtaining the justice he sought was becoming the only reality in his life.

At any rate, when he finally determined that he must, for his own peace of mind, bring the matter to some kind of conclusion, and announced his intention in December 1811 to go to London, he did not tell his wife what his real objective was. Tentative plans were on foot for Mary Stevens to take over the whole of the millinery business, and Bellingham's London trip was ostensibly to make some of the necessary business arrangements with suppliers. It was understood that he also intended to buy iron in the City for his own commercial affairs.

Some of these transactions he did undertake. Mary wrote to him in a cheerful mood on Sunday, 18 January 1812: 'Your letter I received in course and I am glad to relieve your anxiety regarding darling Henry who is wonderfully recovered and has cut two teeth.' She explained an error in an order for silk, and asked him to persist in having it corrected. 'I feel most obliged by your attention in regard to our business, but must request you to call again at Phillips and Davisons as it is their Travellers mistake and not any fault of ours.'

She clearly expected his visit to be brief.

I feel very much surprized at your not mentioning any time for your return, you will be three weeks gone on Thursday, and you know I cannot do anything with regard to settling this Business untill your return. We have got in very little Money since you left . . . I think I need not instruct you to act with economy, your feeling for your family will induce you to do it. I request you to write by return of post. The children send dear Papa . . . an affect^{nte} kiss, with one from Mamma, and I remain yours very affectionately,

MARY BELLINGHAM

She added a postscript: 'Pray let me know when you intend to return, Miss Stevens desires to be remembered' [100].

But Bellingham had no plans for return until the matter was settled, once and for all. He had found lodgings at No. 9, New Millman Street, in the home of a young widow, Rebecca Robarts, where he paid 10s. 6d. a week for rent and 5s. for firing, and started his campaign on 21 January with a memorial to the Prince Regent. It is doubtful whether, for all the premeditation of his final act, he had any intention or thought, in the early stages, of carrying his claims to so deadly a climax. It seems clear that at this time he contemplated nothing more than an all-out paper assault. The justice of his position as he saw it (whether true or nothing more than a figment of his own self-delusion) could not fail to reach a satisfactory conclusion – if only he could get it to the right ears. He may have moderated his original 'wild goose schemes' for getting £100,000: a Dublin paper, after the assassination, quoted recent correspondence with a local merchant in which 'he stated, that he expected to get from Mr Perceval a sum of 5 or 6,000 l.' But some redress he *must* have [101].

His laborious exploration of the channels of authority was infinitely patient, infinitely polite. Bored officials in the Privy Council office, the Treasury and the Home Office read his carefully written communications, submitted them dutifully to their superiors, were given instructions for reply, entered them in departmental minute books, and penned colourless, formal acknowledgements and decisions that closed door after door firmly in the face of the tall, thin, unobtrusive man, who thanked them, and left with few signs of irrational rage or bluster.

February 18, from Mr Under-Secretary John Beckett: 'I am

directed ... to acquaint you, that your Petition to His Royal Highness the Prince Regent, has been referred, by the command of His Royal Highness, for the Consideration of the Lords of His Majesty's Most Honorable Privy Council. I am, Sir, Your most obedient, Humble Servant . . .' [*102*].

From Mr Under-Secretary Beckett, 9 March: 'I am directed ... to acquaint you, that your Petition to His Royal Highness the Prince Regent, praying that he would be pleased to order your Memorial therein inclosed, addressed to the House of Commons, to be brought before Parliament, has been laid before His Royal Highness, and that he was not pleased to signify any commands thereupon . . .'

From Mr Beckett, 20 March: 'I am directed ... to acknowledge the receipt of your letter . . . requesting permission . . . to present your petition to the House of Commons; and in reply I am to acquaint you, that you should address your application to the Right Hon. the Chancellor of the Exchequer.'

It now seemed as if he had come full circle. It was Perceval who, as Chancellor of the Exchequer, had told him nearly two years earlier, in the letter signed by his secretary Thomas Brooksbank, that 'Mr Perceval thinks [it] is not of a nature for the consideration of Parliament'.

He had discussed his case personally with Lord Chetwynd and Mr Buller, Clerks of the Privy Council, and with Mr Litchfield, solicitor for the Treasury, none of whom had given him any warmer comfort. 'At last, then, I was told, I had nothing to expect, and was forced reluctantly to notice, in a more determined manner, the ill-treatment I had received' [*103*].

In this 'more determined manner', he sat down on 23 March and penned a letter 'To Their Worships the Police Magistrates of the Public Office, in Bow-Street':

> Sirs: I much regret its being my lot to have to apply to your Worships under most peculiar and novel circumstances. For the particulars of the case, I refer to the enclosed letter from Mr Secretary Ryder, the notification from Mr Perceval, and my petition to Parliament, together with the printed papers herewith. The affair requires no further remark, than that I consider his Majesty's government to have completely endeavoured to close the door of justice, in declining to have, or

even to permit, my grievances to be brought before Parliament for redress, which privilege is the birthright of every individual.

The purpose of the present, is, therefore, once more to solicit his Majesty's ministers, through your medium, to let what is right and proper be done in my instance, which is all I require. Should this reasonable request be finally denied, I shall then feel justified in executing justice myself – in which case I shall be ready to argue the merits of so reluctant a measure with his Majesty's Attorney-General, wherever and whenever I may be called upon so to do. In the hopes of averting so abhorrent but compulsive an alternative, I have the honour to be, Sirs . . . [104]

Here, had they realized it, was the voice of madness. But these calm, grammatical, understated phrases in Bellingham's clerkly hand aroused no fears. Mr Read, Chief Magistrate of Bow Street, studied the letter and replied in a perfunctory memorandum simply that he had felt it his duty to pass it on to the Secretary of State.

Still reluctant to take drastic action, Bellingham now tried another tack. He called on General Gascoyne, Member for Liverpool, at his London residence, and spent about an hour at a mid-April interview trying to persuade him to bring the petition before Parliament. Gascoyne listened patiently, then recommended that he petition the Ministers, but Bellingham already knew the futility of such an approach. However, to avoid any accusation of avenues left unexplored, he went once more to the Treasury Office. From the neat pages of the departmental records arises a faint odour of long-suffering on the part of Treasury clerks.

Treasury Chambers Minute Book, 21 April:

Read two letters from Mr John Bellingham dated 26th Ult°
& 9th Ins^t together with his Petition claiming redress from
H M's Government on Account of the Losses & Sufferings
experienced by him in consequence of some Criminal Proceedings instituted against him & arising out of Mercantile
Transactions in Russia in 1804 and subsequent Years.

Transmit the Papers to Mr Cooke & desire he will submit
the same to the Consideration of Lord Castlereagh & move

his Lordship to favor this Board with his Opinion whether
the circumstances of this case are such as would warrant the
Interpretation of H M's Government in the manner suggested
by the Memorialist or in any other mode [105].

Treasury Minute, 5 May:

Read Ltre from Mr Cooke (Under Sec^y of State) dated the
29th Ult° on the petition of Mr Jn° Bellingham claiming relief
on account of certain Losses & Sufferings – alledged to have
been experienced by him in consequence of some criminal proceedings instituted against him by the Government of Russia
in the year 1804 – wherein he [Mr Cooke] states by direction
of Lord Castlereagh that it appears upon reference to the
papers in his Lordship's department, that detailed particulars
of Mr Bellingham's case were submitted for the consideration
of Marquis Wellesley in 1809 – and by a Minute attached to
this statement (copy of which he encloses) that a communication was had with Mr Stuart Sec^y to Lord G. L. Gower in
1804 and afterwards H M's Minister at St Petersburgh, and
with Sir Stephen Shairp late British Consul Genl in Russia,
who are well acquainted with the circumstances of the case . . .
    Write to Mr Bellingham acquainting him that upon a refer-
ence to His Majesty's Secretary of State for Foreign Affaires
[sic] it does not appear that this Government could interfere
in his case even if this country were in Amity with Russia
[106].

Someone wrote, as instructed by the minute. 'There was a reply,
refusing his demand, prepared for the signature of one of the
Secretaries of the Treasury,' reported the *Courier* on 13 May, 'and
it would have been signed in the course of Monday, and sent to
him. But it was not signed, and of course he had not received it
when he committed the dreadful act.'
    It would have made no difference, for the die was already cast.
John Beckett, on 18 April, had directed him once again to the
Chancellor of the Exchequer, and Bellingham, recognizing he had
been shunted on to a treadmill, went in person to the office of the
Secretary of State to announce his intention of taking justice into
his own hand. A Mr Hill of that office, having met before with

this kind of threat from disappointed petitioners, told him he was at liberty to take such measures as he thought proper.

No one could have known that Bellingham would take this as a '*carte blanche*, to act in whatever manner I thought proper' [*107*]. From this moment on, he regarded himself as exonerated from all blame.

CHAPTER ELEVEN

I would rather commit suicide

WHILE the petitions and letters had been moving along the conveyor-belt of official routine, Bellingham had been going about his normal business in London, calling on suppliers, talking to customers and clients, attending church, visiting friends and relatives. In Liverpool, searching a drawer one day in the course of her domestic duties, Mary Bellingham had discovered, with other papers, copies of her husband's memorial to the Prince Regent, prepared before his departure for London. She knew now that the tension had not relaxed, and all her fears at once flared up again. She was very much afraid (she wrote apprehensively to Cousin Ann in Southampton, where she was then living) that John was off again on his mad plan. Her husband, moved by her distress but unshaken in his determination, continued his calm, controlled preparations for the disposal of the millinery business as if he were perfectly assured of a successful outcome to his claims.

Mary Stevens was planning a brief visit to London, and on 16 April Bellingham wrote to his wife, rather unwisely combining husbandly affection with a message to Miss Stevens.

My dear Mary, Yours dated the 12th did not reach my hands till yesterday evening – you have acted right in following my instructions, and the rest leave to my solicitude, as can assure you it is not forgotten. I could have wished you had mentioned where and with whom Henry is and to let me know how the dear Boy goes on. Herewith a few lines for Miss S—— – for her government in the Business – and which you may consider as the remainder of your letter.

My dear Miss Stevens: As my affairs in London are terminating according to wish, you may easily imagine its my desire for Mrs B—— to quit the Business as soon as possible, and for you to come into full possession of it. The money that has been put in I do not look to, my family having had the benefit of a maintenance and the outstanding debts I am willing to take upon me. Therefore, when you come to Town, I will accompany you to the respective Trades people for the arrangements so that I do not see any occasion for irksomeness on your part in seeing these folks. Bring the Books and confide in me to do what is right and proper. You will not be deceived . . . I hope to be informed when you mean to be here that I may attend you at the Coach: and command my services in every respect wherein I can be in any way useful to you.

Mary Bellingham was not at all pleased by her husband's news. 'If I could think that the prospects held out in your letter received yesterday were to be realized,' she replied in a letter dated April only, but clearly in reply to the one he had addressed to both Marys, 'I would be the happiest creature existing, but I have been so often disappointed that I am hard of belief. With regard to Miss Stevens going to London . . . before she takes the journey . . . be certain you can *make good* your *intentions*, for should you not ultimately be enabled to fulfill them we would be sunk in ruin from not having sufficient means to meet the tradespeople.'

She also had her own plans for disposing of the business:

'I have not shown Miss Stevens your letter, for should you succeed, I mean with your permission to give up my share in the business to dear Eliza, who is in a distressed situation in New York, as her mother did not leave her a farthing, and she will be obliged to return to her family here. How truly delighted I shall be at having any means of returning her kindness to me and James . . .

Mary was, moreover, more than a little annoyed with her husband. She went on huffily:

> I cannot help remarking that in writing to Miss Stevens you address her in the same manner as me. Oh [it is] my dear Miss Stevens & yours truly John Bellingham. Now I cannot help feeling hurt that there is no distinction made between an indifferent person and an affectionate wife who has suffered so much for you and your children – it appears as if I was no more to you than any woman that you were obliged to write a letter to ... [I have?] a delicate & feeling mind: these are *insults*, more particularly as my indisposition seems to have been forgotten ... The change in my appearance will convince you that I have been very ill, as I am now as thin *as I ever was* ...
>
> If I was to follow your example, *six lines* might fill my letter – but perhaps I am not worthy of more. I shall expect your answer by return of Post, say Thursday: by that time I hope something will be concluded about your affair.

A spirited girl, Mary. She ended the letter with frigid politeness: 'Yours truly, Mary Bellingham' [108].

Up to this moment, only Mary Bellingham and Mary Stevens among those nearest to him had any idea of the sharpening focus of his purpose, and his wife's disapproval of his relentless pursuit of redress could have arisen only from her worries about the consequent inattention to his own business, not from the remotest apprehension of the fearful decision he had made. In the Robarts household at No. 9, New Millman Street, Bellingham was almost a model lodger. He was fond of children, and his young landlady found him helpful, quiet and kind. Once, when one of the children was missing, he proved to be a tower of strength, sparing no effort in tracing and returning the youngster to his home. He frequently accompanied the family to the Sunday church service, and made few demands for attention. The household maidservant, whose name was variously reported as Ann/Catherine/Mary Fidgeon/Fidgins/Pidgin/Fidges/Figgins, thought he was 'a remarkable regular man'. He was highly respected by her mistress and her family [109].

By the end of April, when almost all the Government doors

had been slammed shut, Bellingham began calm, precise and deadly preparations for what he now believed to be the only possibility left open to him. Redress was his due.

> Where a man has so strong and so serious a criminal case to bring forward as mine has been [so his reasoning went] the nature of which was purely national, it is the bounden duty of Government to attend to it, for justice is a matter of right, and not of favour. And when a Minister is so unprincipled and presumptuous at any time, but especially in a case of such urgent necessity, to set himself above both the Sovereign and the Laws, as has been the case with Mr Perceval, he must do it at his personal risk, for, by the law, he cannot be protected [110].

He began to haunt the House of Commons so that he could learn to recognize by sight all the villains in his drama. Perhaps at first he had been uncertain which victim to choose. Around 20 April he went to the shop of a well-known gunsmith, W. Beckwith, at No. 58, Skinner Street on nearby Snow Hill, and bought a pair of strong steel pistols with half-inch calibre, for which he paid four guineas. The pistols were about seven inches long altogether, and had a short screw barrel of little more than two inches. In order to be sure of their firing ability, Bellingham journeyed to Primrose Hill on Hampstead Heath, and practised shooting.

In March he had some dealings with James Taylor, an appropriately named tailor living at No. 11, North Place, Gray's Inn Lane. He had ordered a pair of pantaloons and a striped toilinet waistcoat at that time. Meeting Taylor casually on 25 April on Guilford Street, which crossed the top of New Millman Street, Bellingham invited him home to discuss another small job. Leaving the tailor in the parlour, he went up to his room, and in about ten minutes came down carrying a dark-coloured coat.

'He gave me directions to make him an inside pocket on the left side, so as he could get at it conveniently, he wished to have it a particular depth, he accordingly gave me a bit of paper about the length of nine inches,' Taylor recalled. According to Bellingham's strict instructions, he finished the job and returned the coat the same evening [111].

To all his acquaintances, Bellingham was continuing to behave as he always did. They regarded him, to the end, as a competent businessman and a responsible, dignified gentleman. Mary Stevens, arriving from Liverpool as planned on Wednesday, 6 May, found him controlled and courteous, though – foolishly, she thought – still determined to tilt at Government windmills. He gave her no clue to the distance he had travelled along the road to madness.

Aware, however, of his inflexible determination to continue what his friends regarded as a profitless aberration, she was prepared to take him severely to task. Her privileged position in the household gave her some freedom to express her views, and she may have come with a mandate from the other Mary to try to bring him to his senses [112].

She had found him absent when she called at his lodgings on Thursday evening, but delivered a letter from one John Parton (his solicitor?) in Liverpool, and left a note asking him to call on her next day at the home of a Mrs Barker in Kirby Street, where she was staying. When he arrived there on Friday morning, she told him how badly upset his wife was, as she was also, to discover the true object of his journey to London. She appealed to him on the grounds of his family's needs, pointing to the time he was losing, and the effect on his children's education because of his absence. He only replied mournfully that they could never be happy until the matter was settled.

'You know, Miss Stevens, it is always a matter of dissention between me and Mrs Bellingham.' He was determined to have justice done, he said. 'He should be undeserving the name of a Parent if he did not endeavour to make some provision for his Children.'

There was no point in further argument just then. It was arranged that he should call next day to examine the ledgers she had brought from Liverpool, and to go with her and her hostess to the exhibition in Spring Garden (the Eighth Annual Exhibition of the Society of Painters in Water-Colours). On arrival next day at her lodgings, Bellingham glanced through the books while Miss Stevens went upstairs to dress. Just before setting off together for the exhibition, she asked him again about his claims.

' "I suppose nothing further has transpired?" '

' "Nothing," ' he replied. He had been rather dilatory that week, he said, because of Mary's arrival, ' "but he determined to set about it vigorously on Monday" '. Just how vigorously, perhaps at this point even he did not know.

Having viewed the exhibition, they both returned to Mrs Barker's, where Bellingham collected the ledgers for a proper examination, after calling first at a couple of places on the way, presumably to introduce Miss Stevens to suppliers. She then went out of town for the weekend, and did not see Bellingham again until eleven o'clock on the morning of Monday, 11 May. He dropped in that day to give her a packet containing letters to his wife and John Parton, and at this time Miss Stevens again edged valiantly around the subject of Bellingham's petitions.

' "If there should be a new ministry, would it not retard your concerns – would it not be better to relinquish it than to oppose the powerful so much?" ' she asked him.

He was adamant. ' "I will not. If ministers refuse to do me justice I will do it myself." ' Laying his hand on his heart, he shocked her with his next words. ' "You do not know, Miss Stevens, what I have endured the last six months; I would rather commit suicide." '

She replied in horror, ' "God forbid that you should commit such an act!" ' She had noted how altered his appearance was since she had seen him last in Liverpool. ' "Your countenance shews what you must have suffered." ' She then asked curiously, ' "But how are you to obtain this?" '

' "I will bring it into a criminal court," ' he said. He did not explain further, except to say that he would ' "compel the minister to do him justice, as he was the only one that opposed him" '.

She hoped it would soon be over, Miss Stevens said, so that he could return to his family. He assured her he would do everything possible to bring the affair to an end, ' "as no person was more inclined to be domestically happy than himself" '. He then wished her good morning and a pleasant journey, and departed. The next time she saw him, he had indeed brought the affair to an end. She found him in Newgate, fettered with double irons, and guarded by three keepers.

On Sunday morning, 10 May, Bellingham went with Rebecca Robarts and her young son to the service in the Chapel of the Foundling Hospital on Guilford Street. In the evening, after dining alone, he walked through the rain with Mrs Robarts to the evening service there. On Monday morning, he had a slight argument with the washerwoman about her charge of a shilling for washing his dressing-gown. His laundry accounts were recorded with scrupulous accuracy and neatness in the blue-covered book he had made up. ' "If he had known the price would have been more than eight pence he would have washed the gown himself" ' [*113*].

He spent the morning writing letters, made a brief call at noon to give these to Mary Stevens for delivery, and in the afternoon – his pistols loaded and stowed in their respective pockets – he set off peacefully with Rebecca Robarts and her little boy to see the exhibits at the European Museum. No sign of his grim preparations was apparent to his companions. The weather was fine and clear, and they strolled to their destination along the two miles or so to King Street, St James's. After viewing the pictures, the little party walked back as far as Sydney's Alley, between Coventry Street and Leicester Square, where, shortly before five o'clock, they parted, Mrs Robarts and the boy for home, Bellingham (who had said casually that he had some business to attend to) for Westminster.

When Vickery and Adkins, the Bow Street runners, came storming into her house somewhere between six and seven o'clock, Rebecca Robarts could not believe what they had to tell her. The deed was impossible, she said in stupefaction. Hadn't they all just spent a quiet afternoon looking at pictures? When he had left her, Mr Bellingham had told her he had just been to buy a prayer book [*114*].

CHAPTER TWELVE

A contrivance to delay the administration of justice

THE trial would open at ten o'clock on the morning of Friday, 15 May. In expectation of the crowds that would inevitably collect around the Old Bailey, troops had been placed at strategic locations throughout the city. By seven o'clock a mass of would-be spectators had gathered at the various court entrances hoping to be admitted, including many elegantly dressed ladies of distinguished rank, whose curiosity was greater than the fear of the crowds they would encounter. The *Morning Chronicle* complimented the sheriffs for arranging that admission should be by written order only, with the result that the court, though full, was not in any way overcrowded. Other accounts, however, contradict this cool assessment. The doorkeepers were charging a guinea a seat at seven o'clock: by ten, when at least two thousand people were clogging the streets in and around Newgate, the price had risen to three guineas [115].

The windows of houses on Ludgate Hill and Fleet Street, as well as those directly overlooking the Old Bailey, were filled with observers – mostly women, one pamphlet noted, on whose faces expressions of anxiety and curiosity mingled. There was, in fact, a general belief at the time that 'women were struck by [Bellingham's] fine and manly person. Strange tales of his amorous complexion, whispered abroad, did not weaken that favourable impression' [116].

The Court filled up early. 'So great was the press', the *Courier* reported, 'that a great number of eminent persons of both Houses of Parliament were compelled to intermix indiscriminately with the multitude in the body of the Court.' Among the multitude was Ann Billett, who, having read with pity and horror the newspaper accounts of her cousin's appalling act, had come posthaste to London from her home in Ringwood, near Southampton, to do what she could to support him [117].

At nine, the Marquis Wellesley and other distinguished personages entered to take their seats on the Bench, and at ten the Lord Mayor made his entrance. The Duke of Clarence followed, with the Lord Chief Justice of the Common Pleas (Sir James Mansfield), the Recorder, and the two other judges, Baron (Sir Robert) Graham and Mr Justice (Sir Nash) Grose, seating themselves on either side of the Lord Mayor. The prisoner was immediately brought in and placed at the Bar.

Bellingham had awakened at his usual hour of seven, and in his usual state of calm composure. By eight thirty, however, when he breakfasted, he began to show some signs of stress, though his routine examination by the Newgate surgeon, William Box, earned him the certificate of fitness necessary for any prisoner before he could be brought to the Bar of the Old Bailey. He ate very little, and was not able to keep even that little down. He also burst into a flood of tears, but quickly assured his concerned attendants that his distress was due not to any fears for himself but to an acute realization of the position in which his act must have placed his wife and children. He asked for an orange, which seemed to settle his stomach, and by the time Keeper Newman came shortly before ten to conduct him through the various passages from the prison to the Sessions House, he was entirely composed.

A hairdresser had come to the cell before breakfast to shave him and dress his hair, which was cut very short. He had dressed carefully for the occasion in a brown greatcoat, yellow waistcoat with small stripes of black, and dark nankeen trousers. He seemed momentarily taken aback by the look of deep horror on every face when he first appeared, but recovered at once, and stepped slowly forward into the dock with a deep bow to the Court [118].

The Attorney-General, Sir Vicary Gibbs (his generally uncivil and caustic manner had earned him the nickname of 'Vinegar' Gibbs) was prosecutor for the Crown, assisted by William Garrow, John Gurney, Mr Knapp and Mr Abbott. The trial that followed was, regardless of the guilt or innocence of the prisoner, a travesty – 'the greatest disgrace to English justice', wrote Lord Brougham, looking back on it [119].

It began with a legal hassle when Bellingham's chief counsel, Peter Alley, (the other was Henry Revell Reynolds) rose to ask for a postponement, an application 'founded upon statements which went to shew that the prisoner could be proved to be insane, if sufficient time were allowed for witnesses to appear in his favour'.

The prisoner must first plead, one way or the other, said the Court. Until then, Mr Alley was out of order, it seemed: he could not be heard, despite his plea that the defence rested on the presumption that Bellingham, by reason of insanity, was not capable of pleading.

In the dialogue that ensued, the Crown was implacably determined to allow no leeway to the defence: Alley was assailed by a furious fusillade of interjection from the prosecution [120].

Attorney-General: ' "It is necessary that the Prisoner should be called on in the first place, to say whether he be Guilty or Not Guilty." '

Mr Garrow: ' "When he has done so, then his Counsel may be called to assist him." '

Chief Justice Mansfield: ' "I cannot hear any person as Counsel for the Prisoner, until he has pleaded." '

Mr Justice Grose: ' "We are not to know at present, that the Prisoner has any Counsel." '

Mr Recorder: ' "Nor even that the Prisoner is the man referred to in the indictment." '

The two indictments were then read by the Clerk of the Arraigns, Thomas Shelton, and Bellingham was formally called on to plead. He began, however, with an attempt to explain the difficulty of his position.

' "My Lords – before I can plead to this indictment, I must state, in justice to myself, that by the hurrying on of my trial, I am placed in a most remarkable situation. It so happens, that my prosecutors are actually the witnesses against me. All the documents on which alone I could rest my defence, have been taken from me, and are now in possession of the Crown. It is only two days since I was told by Mr Litchfield, the Solicitor of the Treasury, to prepare for my trial; and when I asked him for my papers, he told me that they would not be given up to me. It is, therefore, my Lords, rendered utterly impossible for me to go into my justification; and under the circumstance in which I find myself, a trial is absolutely useless. The papers are to be given to me after the trial, but how can that avail me for my defence? I am, therefore, not ready for my trial" ' [121].

The indignant Attorney-General jumped up at once to splutter explanations, but was brought abruptly back by the Chief Justice to the point at issue. Had the prisoner yet pleaded? The prisoner had not, and did not wish to at that point. But the insistence of the court won out, and Bellingham now said in a subdued voice, ' "Not guilty. I put myself upon God and my country." '

The Attorney-General was immediately back on his feet to continue his explanations. Yes, the papers had had to be withheld ' "for the purposes of justice" ', but the prisoner had been informed they would be available to him at the trial, and copies provided beforehand if required, on a request from his solicitor. The value of this magnanimous revelation was somewhat lessened by Mr Alley's subsequent statement that ' "it was only yesterday that we (his counsel, Mr Alley and Mr Reynolds) were applied to. I never saw the Prisoner before." '

Alley then offered two affidavits, which were later read to the court by the Clerk, asserting their belief in the prisoner's insanity. The first was from Ann Billett, the second from a Mrs Mary Clarke who lived in Bagnio Court, Newgate Street, each of whom stated her belief that Bellingham had earlier shown strong signs of insanity. Ann explained her years of knowing the prisoner, and added that there were many witnesses from out of town who could testify to his periods of derangement, especially a Captain Barker, an officer in a militia regiment. Mrs Clarke's testimony corroborated Ann's, though she could not speak for more than the last two years.

' "It was only on Monday that the alleged act was said to have been perpetrated." ' Mr Alley went on reasonably. ' "A letter could not have been sent to Liverpool till next day, and it was impossible that any answer could since have been received. Even where a person was to be tried in the town in which he usually resided, some time must be necessary to enable him to provide for his trial" ' [*122*].

The Attorney-General swept these arguments relentlessly aside. ' "It appears that this is clearly a contrivance to delay the administration of justice, and that these witnesses are purposely selected to impose upon the Court a false belief . . . Where has the Prisoner been for these four months preceding this act for which he is this day called upon to answer? . . . Has Mrs Billet, or has Mrs Clerk . . . seen him during that period, so as to witness his conduct? No, my Lords, he has been resident in this town, in the midst of a family, known to multitudes of persons in this town, transacting business in this town, and with as much sagacity and as perfect and masculine an understanding as any man who now hears me [*123*].

' "None of these persons come before you, to give you an account of his state of mind. None of those who can know the fact come forward to state their knowledge of it." ' The Attorney-General swooped down on poor Ann (whose close relationship to Bellingham was never mentioned) and the other witness. " 'It is evidently a contrivance set up by a woman in Southampton" ' – the phrase put Ann into the category of a shameless and self-seeking impostor – ' "and another woman living in this city, whose means of communication with the Prisoner does not appear. It is only they who pretend that he is in an unsound state of mind; but neither of them have attempted to swear that he was in an infirm state of mind about the time that the crime was committed." '

With a disdainful and contemptuous disregard for the facts, 'Vinegar' Gibbs then turned his scorn on Mr Alley. ' "If, indeed, there was any ground for the plea of insanity, or of infirmity of mind, who is the best judge of it, and by whom could it be most satisfactorily proved? Would not his Counsel have sent a person, conversant in such disorders, to examine the Prisoner; some person whose statement your Lordships would have regarded as of deep importance? No such course has been pursued." ' thundered the Attorney-General, knowing full well the restrictions of time forced on his learned friend that had made such an examination impossible, ' "but Affidavits such as I have described, have been put in – evidently not to advance, but to retard and weaken justice." '

Mr Alley had done his best, nevertheless. He explained patiently that he and his colleague Mr Reynolds had in fact applied to ' "two of the ablest and most celebrated men of the present day (Drs Simmons and Munro); one of whom stated that it was impossible for him to appear this day, and the other returned no answer" '.

Both doctors were, indeed, in the forefront of psychiatric practice of the day, and both had attended George III on occasion. Illness may have been Dr Samuel Foart Simmons's reason for refusing Alley's request, as he died the following year. No reason for the failure of Dr Thomas Munro to make any reply at all was ever offered. In the context of today's legal requirements, the airy and cavalier acceptance that proper medical opinion could be dispensed with shocks the modern mind.

Mr Reynolds now rose to add a comment, but was silenced by the Recorder, who told him that he had no right to speak at that point. Then, after a few moments of deliberation by the court, Chief Justice Mansfield announced that, no good reason having been advanced for postponement, the trial would proceed.

'If there were proper grounds advanced for postponing the Trial, he would coincide with the application – but no such grounds could be discovered in the Affidavits. They were both perfectly silent as to the conduct of the Prisoner since his residence in London – they were both silent as to his demeanour for months and months past, nay, for years. The first spoke of Liverpool as the Prisoner's established residence: the second related to his return from Russia two years ago. Now, could it be supposed that he went, or would be permitted to go to Russia, if he were in a disordered state of mind?'

The jury was then empanelled, after predictable challenges, and the Attorney-General opened with a speech both lengthy and searing, its fire directed at the only defence that had been suggested, the assumption of Bellingham's insanity.

'With regard to the previous life the Prisoner had led, he [the Attorney-General] had nothing to do with it, except in so far as it was concerned with the present prosecution. The Prisoner was a merchant. He was in business for himself, and had shewed that he was a man of sense, capable, not only of carrying on his own business, but that he was even employed in conducting the business of others . . . He was left to manage his own affairs, none of his friends interfering to prevent him. Not only, however, was he left to manage his own affairs, but he was even entrusted with the management of the affairs of others. There was not even an idea of any taint or blemish in his capacity in this respect.'

(Could this astute businessman ever have been the bankrupt tinplate-worker of Oxford Street, one wonders?)

The Attorney-General continued hammering home his point.

'There was no pretence for supposing the prisoner to be what in law is termed *non compos mentis*. He managed not only his own affairs but the affairs of others; and there was not the slightest pretence or suspicion that his mind was not perfectly sound and right . . .'

He then explained to the jury the difference between civil and criminal incapacity.

'A man might be in such a state of incapacity, as to be inadequate to the management of his own affairs; or might even have the management of them taken out of his hands; but a person so situated was not thereby discharged from his criminal acts . . . A man, though incapable of conducting his civil affairs, is criminally liable, provided he has a mind capable of distinguishing between right and wrong.'

He brought forward two earlier cases to illustrate his arguments. In the one, incapacity to manage his own affairs had been proved; in the other, insanity had been supported by medical opinion. Yet both the accused were adjudged capable of distinguishing between right and wrong, and both were executed. Was Bellingham, the shrewd businessman who had shown no such incapacity, no such erratic behaviour, less competent, less sane, with his coldly planned arrangements, than these?

The Attorney-General reiterated,

'Here there was no deficiency of understanding. The Prisoner was not only capable of managing, and did actually manage his own affairs, but he also managed the affairs of others. The question therefore for the Jury to consider in this case was, whether the Prisoner at the Bar was, or was not, capable of distinguishing between right and wrong, at the time when the crime for which he was now called on to answer, was perpetrated by him?'

Bellingham listened to the attack with an appearance of the utmost serenity. While standing, he had 'frequently looked round and appeared to contemplate the crowd with a curious eye'. At one point he took an orange from his pocket and ate it during a pause in the proceedings. After a while, he asked for a chair, which was at once brought. Entirely at ease, once seated, he amused himself with the leaves strewn along the front of the Bar, rolling them in his fingers, twisting the sprigs of rue and sometimes smelling them, while the Crown heard the testimony of its witnesses [124].

One by one the witnesses added their contribution to the mosaic until the picture emerged. Former witnesses repeated their stories, new witnesses came to fill gaps. Once again William Smith told of lifting the dying Prime Minister from the floor and carrying him to the office of the Speaker's secretary (William Smith would have another link with the famous in later years when he had a grandchild named Florence Nightingale); Dr Lynn testified to the cause of death; Henry Burgess described his appropriation of the pistol and the other items from the prisoner's pockets. General Gascoyne explained how his position in the committee room upstairs, close to a door opening directly on to the landing, had enabled him to hear the shot instantly and clearly, and started him on the impetuous rush that ended with his violent seizure of the prisoner.

The well-named tailor, James Taylor, told of the commission he had received from Bellingham to make a special pocket inside his coat on the left side. The coat was produced, identified by John Newman, the Newgate Keeper, as the one in which the prisoner had arrived at the prison, and further identified by Newman's assistant George Bowman (or Beaumont).

'I was in the room when the prisoner acknowledged this coat to be his coat; he said that in the scuffle at the lobby in the House of Commons the coat was torn, and that he wished

to have it mended, it had been torn by some person endeavouring to take the papers from his pocket; he wished to have
a taylor to mend the coat; there was a man in the chapel yard
in the room under the prisoner's room, that was a taylor, and
the coat was lowered down to him by a string to the window
to be mended.'

John Norris repeated his version of the events in the lobby,
Dowling identified the pistol found in Bellingham's pocket. The
Bow Street runner, John Vickery, recounted his orders to search
Bellingham's room.

'He was sent to search the Prisoner's lodgings on Monday
last, and in a drawer, in his bedroom upstairs, he found bags
for a brace of pistols, a small powder flask, some gunpowder
in a paper box, four bullets in a bag, and some small flints in
a paper, together with a pistol key, and a mould for casting
bullets. On the witness applying the balls to the pistol produced by Mr Burgess, he found that they fitted exactly; two
of them had been before screwed into the pistol.'

This, with one or two more short interrogations to prove a necessary point, was the case for the Crown. ' "Prisoner," ' said the Lord
Chief Justice, ' "the evidence being gone through on the part of the
prosecution, now is the time for you to make any defence you
have to offer or to produce any witnesses that you wish to be
examined" ' [125].

CHAPTER THIRTEEN

My mind was in a state of horror

WHAT witnesses? he might well have asked. At first, Bellingham did not hear the Chief Justice's statement. When it was repeated, he rose to his feet and replied simply, ' "I leave it to my counsel, my Lord." ' He received a reply that might have daunted another man. Counsel was allowed, he was told, only to examine witnesses and to advise him on points of law. Otherwise, his defence was in his own hands – a law (not changed until 1837) that placed most prisoners at a formidable disadvantage.

Bellingham, however, was equal to the task. The fluency of his speech and the firm tone in which it was delivered drew much comment from observers. He began by asking once again for his papers: copies, if they had been supplied as the Attorney-General had stated, had clearly proved inadequate. Before delivery could be made, it was necessary to call Joseph Hume to produce them and General Gascoyne to verify that they were in fact the papers taken from the prisoner, ' " exactly in the same state as when he obtained them, excepting that they had been numbered" ' [*126*].

Bellingham spent some moments, after removing the red tape, in looking through the documents before beginning to speak. It was soon evident that he was not interested in a defence based on insanity. In fact, he actually thanked the Attorney-General for

his spirited denial of any such possibility. He admitted the act:
justification for it was what he set out to prove; and in this, had
not ' "burning indignation at the crime absorbed all compassion for
the criminal" ', his judges might have seen the evidence of the
madness they denied [127]. Facing the jury, Bellingham now
began a speech that continued for a full two hours. It was remarked that though the papers sometimes trembled in his hands,
this seemed to come from his anxiety to put across the justice of
his case rather than from any apprehension about his fate.

> 'Gentlemen of the Jury: I feel I am under great obligations
> to the learned Attorney-General for inducing the Court to
> dismiss the objection that was made by my Counsel on the
> ground of insanity; because it is by far more fortunate for me
> that such a plea should be determined to be unfounded, than
> that it should be established. At the same time I must express
> my gratitude to my Counsel, whose object was certainly most
> meritorious. That I am insane I certainly am perfectly ignor-
> ant, and I assure you that I never had an idea of it, with the
> exception of one instance in Russia, where my insanity was
> made a matter of public notoriety.'

Here he paused, in one of the few moments of embarrassment
that overtook him.

> 'Gentlemen, I beg pardon for thus detaining you, but I am
> wholly unaccustomed to situations like the present, and this
> is the first time I ever addressed a public audience; I therefore
> hope to receive your candid indulgence, and trust that you
> will pay more attention to the matter detailed than to the
> manner in which it is delivered.'

He was, if he might use the phrase, a ' "compulsive volunteer" ' to
this Bar: having voluntarily committed the deed, certainly, but
compelled to it by circumstances.

> 'Do you suppose me the man to go with a deliberate design,
> without cause or provocation, with a pistol, to put an end to
> the life of Mr Perceval? No, Gentlemen! far otherwise. I have
> strong reasons for my conduct, however extraordinary;

reasons which when I have concluded, you will acknowledge to have fully justified me in this fatal fact. Had I not possessed these imperious excitements, and had murdered him in cold blood, I should consider myself a monster, not only unfit to live in this world, but too wicked for all the torments that may be inflicted in the next.'

He then unwound to them the long reel of his sufferings, reading his fruitless petitions one by one, and their formal, rejecting replies. For most of the time his voice was firm, level and unimpassioned, setting the disastrous events in cold and reasoned sequence. Sometimes his emotions overcame him.

'Reflect now, Gentlemen, if you can imagine yourselves in a state of such accumulated misery, what must have been your feelings, and from thence judge of mine. I had been but recently married to a wife then only twenty years of age, with an infant at her breast, and pregnant with a second child; yet I was doomed to continue immured in a dungeon for six months longer . . .'

He burst into tears, and could not speak for some moments.

'On my arrival in Petersburgh, what was it fit that I should do? What you or any man would have done under such circumstances. I felt myself injured in my fortune, and above all, in my reputation. Should I not go to the Minister of Justice for the vindication of my honour? . . .
'Count Kotzebue had the affair investigated in most of the departments at Archangel, and finding my statement accurate, he gave me a document which enabled me to bring my case before the Senate, that a full and fair investigation might take place . . . Just at this period Lord Gower arrived, and I put the papers into his hands, that they might be laid before the Senate. I continued with Mrs Bellingham during that time, she being then at St Petersburgh, which I had then reached. Before the Senate I produced my complaints, but before any decision was had, I found myself arrested on two charges, the one criminal, and the other civil; and I was dragged from my family, thrown again into prison, where I continued for no less a space than two years!

'These were trials that would bow the proudest head, and sink the noblest heart. Think, Gentlemen, what I endured and what was my offence? Nothing: there was not the shadow of proof against me ... It was falsehood from beginning to end; yet this they called giving me justice. This, thank God! is not the way it is administered in this happy country.'

He was overcome with emotion at this point.

'Gentlemen, I feel myself so much exhausted, that I must beg to pause for a few seconds.'

He delayed so long, weeping quietly, that Mansfield had to call on him to continue.
He went on:

'Gentlemen, thus was I again thrown into a dungeon and into despair ... The very day I expected a complete enfranchisement; the very hour I looked for re-established honour and reviving fortunes, I was handed to another prison, because I would not and could not submit to the extortion of two thousand roubles.'

His memories of those indignities and deprivations were vivid and painful in his mind.

'I was dragged about the streets with offenders who had been guilty of the most atrocious crimes ... Of what must my heart have been composed, that was the sufferer of this indignity, and this torture, to the eternal disgrace of both nations? I applied to Sir Stephen Shairpe again without success – I was not listened to – I could obtain no redress there. I sought it here, in my native country, I have been again refused! My fortune and my character have been ruined, and I stand here alone and unprotected by all but the laws of my country. They, I trust, will afford me that which all others have denied. ...'

He now made public his specific accusations against the British Government for the failure of its representatives to come to his support.

'All this could not have happened but by the connivance of
Lord L. Gower, and Sir S. Shairpe. During this period, too,
Mrs Bellingham, then in a state of pregnancy, and one infant
in her arms, was anxiously waiting for me to accompany her
to England: I could not; and she was compelled to perform
that dangerous voyage alone, and unprotected, though in a
condition so interesting, while Lord Gower saw, and permitted so much misery.

'Oh, my God!' [cried the prisoner, overcome]. 'What must
his heart be made of? Gentlemen, I appeal to you as men, as
fathers, as Christians, if I had not cause of complaint . . .'

He burst into tears, and once again had to stop until he had
recovered his composure. Ann Billett, among the spectators in
the body of the court, must have been heart-sick as she watched
the agony in that known, familiar face.

He continued:

Finding I was too firm to bend to their views, they then
proclaimed me a bankrupt, allowing me, according to the
law of Russia, only three months to settle every claim upon
me. And such was the eagerness of the Chamber of Commerce to ruin me, that they employed emissaries to enquire
out persons to whom I owed money: their clerks stopped
people in the streets, and asked them, "Do you know Mr Bellingham? Does he owe you any money? Do you know he is
a bankrupt, and that he is going to England with all his
property?" and other similar questions.'

Such public humiliation would sear the very soul of a man of
Bellingham's touchy pride. With satisfaction, he said,

'Yet after all, they were obliged to give a document, testifying that there were neither claimants nor creditors. These
documents I afterwards placed in the hands of Marquis
Wellesley, and I call upon the Noble Marquis, whom I see in
the Court, to disprove this assertion, if it be false.'

The Noble Marquis remained silent. The prisoner continued,
explaining the repeated failure of British representatives in Russia
to come to his aid.

'Gentlemen, while I relate this, I must say, it would have been fortunate for me, and it would have been more fortunate for Mr Perceval, had Lord Gower received the ball which terminated the life of the latter gentleman.'

A murmuring in the Court of disapproval and disgust that followed this statement seemed to disconcert Bellingham. It seems clear from his comments that his intended victim had never been Lord Gower, once he had made his choice. It had been the Prime Minister as head of the Administration. At no time had Bellingham intended his act as revenge – only, as he saw it, justice. He was suffering, he considered, ' "merely because it was Mr Perceval's pleasure that justice should not be granted" '.

Mansfield asked him had he finished. No, he had more yet to say. The Court and the absorbed spectators now followed him from door to Government door as rejection came on the heels of rejection. When he told of his application to Perceval as Chancellor of the Exchequer, he gave his words 'a strong and peculiar emphasis'. He read aloud the reply from Perceval, signed by Thomas Brooksbank. ' "I was informed, that the time for receiving private petitions was past for that Session; nor," ' he added, " 'did he think my claims such as could with propriety be submitted to Parliament" '.

Bellingham explained.

'Now with regard to private Bills, I know there is a limited time for their reception. But I have yet to learn, that a private petition, imploring justice from the wisdom and integrity of Parliament, could ever be out of time. Justice is a matter of right, and not of favour; and, as such, I think it should be dispensed at all times. If I am wrong in this opinion, there are many Honourable Members now present in the Court who can correct me ... Where can an injured subject appeal so justly as to Parliament? and if that constitutional door be shut against him, where is his redress?'

Here was the core of his reasoning. What, if constitutional methods failed, was left to him to do to gain his justice?

'By this refusal I was again reduced to despair. My situation became daily and hourly worse. My property was all sold;

my creditors were clamorous; my family was ruined; my mind was in a state of horror.'

Still, he said, he had gone on doggedly making lawful applications.

'Such, Gentlemen, continued to be my forlorn condition. My prayers were rejected whenever offered . . . I was sinking under the pressure of accumulated miseries – miseries brought on, not by my own indiscretion, but by the injustice of others. The Attorney-General has told you, and he has told you truly, that till this period my name – my character, were without a blemish; till this melancholy, this deplorable transaction, which no man, I can solemnly assure you, laments more deeply than I do – till this fatal moment, my life was without reproach.'

His voice broke as he spoke, and again he burst into tears. He had spoken truly enough. He did, indeed, lament the death of his victim, but neither then nor at any time did he accept the blame for it. His hand was the instrument indeed – but instrument only of the injustices that drove him to the deed.

'That my arm destroyed him, I allow; that he perished by my hand, I admit; but to constitute felony, there must be *malice prepense*, there must be the wilful intention, and I deny that it has been proved. Unless proved, however, the felony cannot be made out; this you will shortly hear from the Bench, and in that case you must acquit me . . .'

He then sat down, clearly disturbed and in tears, and asked for a glass of water. The exertion and emotional strain of the past two hours showed in his flushed face, and in his hair, which was soaked with sweat; but he sat still, the internal agitation that rocked him kept under visibly tight control [*128*].

Had the judges not been almost criminally prejudiced, Bellingham's incredible argument – that to shoot and kill the representative of those he saw as oppressors was the ultimate right in law remaining to one denied what he had personally defined as due justice – would have been its own manifest evidence of insanity. But (a lawyer would write forty years later):

the more calmly and firmly that the unhappy prisoner spoke, detailing his grievances with such a lively retrospect of endurance as to weep bitterly during the enumeration, though his hearers listened unmoved – justifying, almost glorying in the deed – the more hardened became a jury unaccustomed to the development of insanity; and, so far as speech could avail a foregone conclusion, the prisoner sealed his own doom [129].

Peter Alley and his colleague Henry Reynolds must have realized the futility of expecting success from any defence that could now be brought. The array of other witnesses Bellingham had wanted to call – Lord Gower, Sir Stephen Shairp, consular and embassy officials from Russia, all those who had signed the letters of rejection – could have done him nothing but harm, though in a note penned the night before his execution he would severely blame his counsel for their failure to let these witnesses be heard. Their evidence could only add the emphasis of premeditation to each step he had taken along the road to murder. The Marquis Wellesley, who had been challenged by Bellingham to deny, if he could, receiving the Russian document exonerating him from bankruptcy, was given no opportunity to answer, and perhaps had nothing to say: whether because such a document had never existed except in a deranged mind, or whether, if it existed in fact, no legal method of redress had been available.

Nevertheless, Alley and Reynolds did their best. Limited by the impossible restrictions that had denied them time to prepare a case, they called the only witnesses who might do any good, Ann Billett, Mary Clarke, and the housemaid at No. 9, New Millman Street [130].

So valiant, loving Ann – this 'woman from Southampton' – took the stand, facing the weight of disapproval in all those intimidating faces, and did her best for her cousin. She was observed to be 'under the strongest impressions of grief and horror' as she told of the impetuous journey that had brought her to London last night from Southampton, 'from a conviction that she knew more of him than any other friend'. She told of their childhood together, of his father's death from insanity, of his many visits to her home in London and hers to his in Duke Street, Liverpool, when his constant brooding on his sufferings had worried them all. She told of his wild dreams of wealth and estates in the country, and the embarrassing visit to the Secretary of State's office. She told of the distress she and Mary had suffered, watching his obsession grow to a point where any mention of Russia threw him into a passion, and how all his friends learned to avoid any mention of the subject.

She was torn to shreds.

'Can you state any period for a month, a week, or a single day, he was ever restrained?' – 'No.'

'Has he been left to act upon his own will as much as me, or any body else?' – 'Yes, I believe he was.'

'After your visit to Mr Smith, at the Secretary of State's office, he remained in town, and after that, neither you nor his wife gave any intimation to Mr Smith that he was a deranged man, or to any officers of government?' – 'No.'

'How long is it ago since you saw him? – 'More than a twelve month ago.'

'Did you ever know him confined for a single day?' – 'No.'

Ann was defeated. Mary Clarke fared no better.

'He came up from Liverpool to London, he came up alone?' – 'Yes . . . he came up alone, to the best of my knowledge, he told me that he was come on business.'

'He transacted business for himself then, did not he?' – 'I do not know any thing about his business.'

'You do not know any body that transacted business for him, do you?' – 'No, I heard that he was confined in Russia.'

'For all that, he was suffered to go about here in this country?' – 'I do not know of any controul over him.'

'Or do you know of any medical person being consulted about him?' – 'No, I do not know.'

'You do not know of any precautions that were taken to prevent him from squandering his property, in this state of derangement, do you?' – 'I do not.'

'You do not know of any course pursued to him by his friends, that would not be pursued to any rational man?' – 'I do not.'

Bellingham's landlady, Rebecca Robarts, though subpoenaed, was too ill to attend: overcome, no doubt, by the unexpected notoriety and the descent on her home of a whole array of great personages and officials, including Magistrate and Member of Parliament Harvey Christian Combe. In her stead, the housemaid, Anne/Catherine/MaryFidgeon/Fidgins/Pidgins/Fidges/Figgins, did her feeble best for the lodger she seems to have liked.

Mr Bellingham was a nice, quiet gentleman, much liked and respected by the family, no trouble to anyone, but she ' "thought he seemed confused, and was so for some time" '. He appeared to have a good deal of business, and wrote a lot of letters.

' "On the Monday, before you went out, had you noticed any-thing particular?" ' – ' "I noticed a word and his actions. I thought he was not so well as he had been for some time past." '

' "Did you ever know of any surgeon or apothecary attending him?" ' All she could answer was, ' "No".' When asked about the pistols, she said she had not known that he had owned any.

Peter Alley, now desperate, went to peer out through the door of the courtroom, in case any of the Liverpool witnesses had by good fortune arrived, and asked the doorkeeper to call, but no one answered. A surge of hope, quickly dashed, lifted his spirits when, a few moments later, Sheriff Heygate informed the Bench that two men had just arrived from Liverpool in a post-chaise and four, to speak on the prisoner's behalf. But when they were brought in to look at Bellingham, they both declared that ' "he was not the person they had supposed him to be, [who was] a person bearing his description, in whose conduct they had seen frequent marks of derangement" ' [131].

Lord Chief Justice Mansfield now summed up the evidence, his comments almost a foregone conclusion. Perhaps it is unfair to suspect that his bursts of tears and broken voice at every mention of Perceval and his fate were deliberately introduced to influence the jury. Certainly they affected most of the spectators, who joined in the weeping. He was doubtless correct, both legally and morally, in his general judgement.

' "If a man fancied he was right, and in consqeuence conceived that if that fancy was not gratified, that he had a right to obtain justice by any means which his physical strength gave him, there was no knowing where so pernicious a doctrine might end" ' [132].

Mansfield's prejudice was demonstrated by his refusal either to accept a plea of insanity or to allow postponement of the trial for the production of witnesses, which earned him criticism both then and later. ' "Some human creatures were void of all power of reasoning from their birth," ' said the Lord Chief Justice, and, ' "such could not be guilty of any crime".' In Bellingham's case, ' "the single question was, whether, at the time this fact was committed, he possessed a sufficient degree of understanding to distinguish good from evil, right from wrong, and whether murder was a crime not only against the law of God, but against the law of his country." '

It might have been argued that Bellingham, whose every word of twisted logic had demonstrated a total inability to see his act as wrong in any way, had placed himself clearly in the very category that should have defined him as insane. The jury, impressed only by the careful preparations to commit murder in what they saw as the deliberate choice of wrong over right by a sane and rational man, thought otherwise. After whispering together in the box for a couple of minutes, they asked permission to retire, and were escorted to the jury-room by an officer of the Court. It took them less than fifteen minutes to return a verdict of guilty.

CHAPTER FOURTEEN

By the neck till you are dead

BELLINGHAM had fully expected acquittal. He had looked closely and steadily at each juror as they all filed out to the jury-room, his expression confident and complacent. Even while the judge was giving his summation, he had whispered to his solicitor, James Harmer, who sat nearby, that he should be sure not to miss sending a note by the evening post to Liverpool, to tell his wife he was free.

He gave the same intent stare at the returning jury, and probably saw his fate in their faces, as did everyone else in the court. There was a total silence as the foreman 'in a faultering voice' announced the verdict of *guilty*. Bellingham's steely self-control, except for a momentary upward rush of blood, kept every expression but surprise from his face. He made no reply when asked if he had anything to say why sentence of death should not be passed upon him. It was about a quarter past six when the Recorder rose to read the sentence, in a speech that swamped the prisoner in a spate of dire adjectives and 'bathed many of the auditors in tears':

'Prisoner at the bar! You have been convicted by a most attentive and a most merciful jury, of one of the most malicious and atrocious of crimes it is in the power of human nature to perpetrate . . . A crime which, although thus heinous in itself, in your case has been heightened by every possible feature of aggravation. You have shed the blood of a man admired for every virtue which can adorn public or private life . . . By his death . . . the country [has lost] one of its brightest ornaments – a man whose ability and worth was likely to produce lasting advantages to this empire, and ultimate benefit to the world . . . Your impure hand has deprived of existence a man as universally beloved, as pre-eminent for his talents and excellence of heart . . . Assassination is most horrid and revolting to the soul of man, inasmuch as it is calculated to render bravery useless, and cowardice successful . . . Your disgraced and indignant country, by the example of your ignominious fate, will appreciate the horror of your offence . . . Sincerely do I hope that the short interval that has elapsed since the commission of this atrocious offence has not been unemployed by you in soliciting that pardon from the Almighty which I trust your prayers may obtain . . . It only now remains for me to pass the dreadful sentence of the law, which is –

'That you be taken on Monday next, to a place of execution, there to be hung by the neck till you are dead, and your body delivered over to be anatomized; and may God have mercy on your soul!' [133]

Though the listeners in the court may have been bathed in tears, Bellingham received the Recorder's elocution with little sign of emotion. He as much as anyone, he had said, regretted the death of Perceval. He did not need to be reminded that a noble man had been removed from among the living. But, though he now discovered he would have to die for it, justice as he saw it had been grimly served. By Perceval's death, he felt he had been granted a kind of redress. He said faintly, ' "My Lord –" ', as if he had something to say to the judge, but Mr Newman informed him that this was not a time for any comment, and led him from the dock. He stumbled a little on the slope of the floor, but did nothing that could be interpreted as emotion at his fate. The crowd that had assembled around Newgate and the Old Bailey received the news almost without a sound. A few huzzas went up as Sir Francis Burdett drove off in his carriage; otherwise, the people quietly and peaceably dispersed. Bellingham's own dignity seemed to have silenced everyone.

In the emptying courtroom a certain amount of argument over the ultimate disposal of the exhibits had erupted among the lawyers and other officials, who all wanted souvenirs. William Jerdan managed to retain the opera glasses (still in his possession as late as 1852 and probably until his death in 1869), also a copy in Bellingham's handwriting, bearing the initials of Joseph Hume, of the assassin's petition of 21 January 1812. This he presented to his friend Sir Francis Freeling, Secretary of the Post Office, together with an outline of the pistol drawn on paper and a plan of the lobby and its occupants [*134*].

A sharp altercation developed between Sheriff Samuel Birch and the Solicitor to the Treasury, Charles Litchfield, when the latter took possession of the pistols. He had already stowed them away in his bag when a furious Birch rushed up to insist loudly on his prerogative of taking custody of all property belonging to prisoners convicted of felonies in that Court and forfeit to the Crown. Litchfield agreed that the Crown had ownership, but denied that Birch was the proper person to hold the pistols; he therefore refused flatly to give them up, and the argument continued to be heated until 'Vinegar' Gibbs, the Attorney-General, intervened to assure the Sheriff ' "they would be disposed of in the proper manner" ' [135].

Together with the remainder of the exhibits, the weapons were eventually lodged in the Secretary of State's office. It may be safely assumed, therefore, that the pistol exhibited later that month at Greenwich Fair (to see which the owner of the booth – who said he had bought it for an immense sum – was charging sixpence admission) was not the one that fired the fatal shot.

No more authentic was the hat viewed by a gentleman in 1891 'at the recent Guelph Exhibition' listed in the catalogue, he said, as Item 1612A: 'Hat worn by the Right Hon. Spencer Perceval when he was shot by Bellingham in the lobby of the House of Commons, May 11, 1812, and showing where it was pierced by the bullet' [*136*]. The pistol, this correspondent claimed, was also exhibited (as Item 1612B) by the Earl of Egmont.

The town was quiet that Friday evening. A play at the Theatre Royal, by Theodore Hook, advertised earlier in the week as *Killing No Murder*, was performed as planned, but had its title hastily

1. The Right Honourable Spencer Perceval

IOHN BELLINGHAM,
the
ASSASSIN.

I certify this to be a strong likeness

Jn.º A Newman
Keeper of Newgate

Drawn by Permission in Court by W.ᵐ Medland

Published as the Act Directs by W. Medland.
Marshall's Nº 5 Suffolk Street Charing Cross

The ASSASSINATION of Mr. PERCIVAL.

Two contemporary engravings

Mr PERCEVAL Assassinated in the Lobby of the House of Commons by JOHN BELLINGHAM. May 11th 1812

DRAWN & ETCHED BY J. T. SMITH.

NORTH VIEW OF THE CITY OF WESTMINSTER (taken in Sept.r 1807) FROM THE ROOF OF THE BANQUETING-HOUSE, WHITEHALL.

This interesting print not only shews the relative connexion of the principal Buildings with a view of Lambeth Palace & the Thames, but
gives a full display of the improvements made about 1757, by the erection of Parliament Street, as a more spacious avenue to the Houses of Lords and
Commons than the former dirty route through King-Street.

London Published as the Act directs Jan.y 25, 1808, by John Thomas Smith N.º 4 Polygon Somers Town

5a. House of Commons

5b. House of Lords, c. 1809

6a and b. William Heygate and Samuel Birch, sheriffs 1812. Both were later Lord Mayors of London, Heygate (who was knighted) in 1822, Birch in 1814.

6c. Jane Perceval (miniature by Andrew Plimer)

6d. William Jerdan, journalist, first to seize the assassin

6e. William Smith, M.P. for Norwich, at whose feet the Prime Minister fell

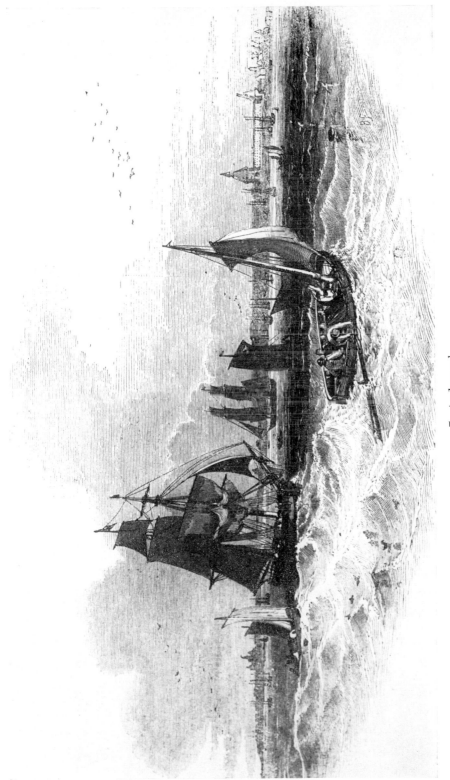

7. Archangel

Bellingham seized on the Frontiers of Russia.

Page

A Travelling Sledge.

9. The Foundling Hospital [top] established on Guilford Street, London, in 1745, by Thomas Coram, whose chapel [below] John Bellingham attended twice on the day before the assassination. The site is now a children's playground, but the colonnades still exist

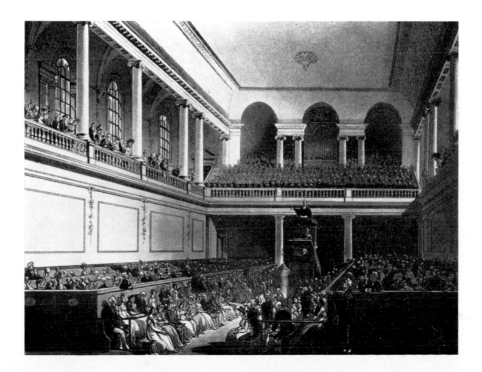

10. St Petersburg

11a. The Old Bailey

11b. John
Bellingham

13. 'Condemned cell' in which Bellingham spent his last two days of life

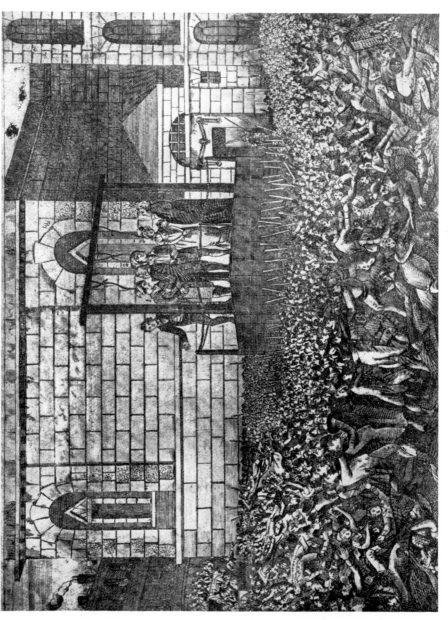

14. The execution of Owen Haggerty and John Holloway (with Elizabeth Godfrey, a murderess) outside Newgate in 1807, at which several people were crushed to death by the crowd. The Ordinary on this occasion was Dr Forde, who also attended Bellingham on the scaffold

15. The Reverend Daniel Wilson (later Lord Bishop of Calcutta)

immediate redress, as the affair ought to have been arranged some years before the difference broke out, and was continued solely at the expence of his personal sufferings — Under these circumstances Petitioner earnestly prays that Your Lordships will take his case into your benign consideration, in order that he be reimbursed such losses as he has actually sustained, or whatever Your Lordships may deem proper, he will then be enabled to organize his affairs, and resume his mercantile functions.

John Bellingham

53 Theobalds Road
February 16th. 1810

16a. A sample of Bellingham's
handwriting

16b. Sir Francis Burdett (said to be
like John Bellingham in appearance)

changed by order of the Lord Chamberlain, and went on as *Buskin and Belvi*. Lady Hertford, the Regent's latest love, postponed the grand rout she had planned to hold. 'In some respects wise,' wrote the Honourable Mrs Robinson to her nephew Lord Fitzharris, 'it is the day of Bellingham's trial, and doubtless she is well advised. The drawing-room and the Prince's levee are both put off' [137].

Bellingham himself, in the condemned cell, remained as composed as ever. He had been conducted not to his former cell, but to one of fifteen reserved for condemned prisoners, which he now inspected with interest. These, ranged on three floors, were all vaulted, nearly nine feet high and measuring approximately nine feet by six. A small double-barred window in the upper wall, about thirty by fourteen inches, let in light and air. The door was of wood, four inches thick, studded with broad-headed nails, and having a tiny circle cut to allow cross-ventilation. When occupied by the prisoner, the two keepers assigned to prevent any inclination to suicide, and any of the numerous visitors who trooped in to see him over the next two days, the cell must have been more than a little crowded [138].

He made no complaint about anything; on the contrary, he expressed polite gratitude for any of the courtesies extended. On entering, he had asked the turnkey to bring him some tea; but, on being informed that the law allowed prisoners, once condemned, nothing but bread and water for their remaining hours of life, he drank without protest from the pitcher of water already in the cell, and ate a good deal of the bread that was immediately brought to him. He would be happy, he said, when he was ' "out of existence" '; and then went to bed and slept until morning, though he was observed from time to time to start violently, as if from a bad dream [139].

Most people had been aghast at Bellingham's reasoning.

> He considered himself as a kind of citizen of nature, as the judge of his own cause, the assessor of his own damages, and the vindicator of his own wrong. 'I have sustained an injury from the Russian Government; I have a right to redress – my own country will not attend to my complaint; they dismiss it, either as not understanding it, or as setting their faces

against it – therefore Mr Perceval must be assassinated' –
Good heavens, what logic is this? . . .

cried *Bell's Weekly Messenger* on Sunday, 17 May.

However, the consciences of a good many people were suffering
twinges of uneasiness about the haste with which the trial had
been rammed through, though most of them agreed with the
verdict.

Samuel Romilly wrote in his diary next day:

> No person can have heard what the conduct and demean-
> our of this man have been since he committed the crime, or
> can have read his defence, without being satisfied that he is
> mad . . . There certainly has been no acting in that calmness
> and steadiness of opinion uniformly manifested by him, that
> what he has done was perfectly justifiable, and that he has set
> an example which will be highly useful to mankind [*140*].

Yet even Romilly, so passionately dedicated to reform of the
code of criminal punishment, felt that this kind of madness 'probably, for the security of mankind, ought not to exempt a man from
being answerable for his actions' – though he thought the trial
would have been better postponed for a few days.

Lord Holland recalled some years later:

> Such hurry was by many thought harsh and illegal, and by
> more injudicious and improper. Insanity, or at least insanity
> of a certain sort, by the law of England exempts the accused
> from a verdict of guilty. The wisdom of such mercy may
> reasonably be questioned; but whatever the law wisely or
> unwisely admits to be a vindication of the act, the accused
> should be allowed full opportunity of proving in his defence
> [*141*].

Witnesses from Liverpool did, in fact, come clattering in, too
late, but whether they brought evidence for or against the prisoner
is not clear. 'Mr Statham of Liverpool came up express with 3
Witnesses and the enclosed papers which the Mayor of L thought
would be material in the trial of Bellingham,' wrote T.B.(?) to an
unnamed correspondent next morning. 'He arrived at the Old

Bailey as the Jury retired from the Box – and finding he was too late to be of service did not notify that he was there.'

To which side he would have been of service is not clear. The later part played by Statham, who was Town Clerk of Liverpool, in trying to alleviate Mary Bellingham's distress, may tend to support a view that the papers were directed to proving Bellingham's insanity and thus saving his life. On the other hand, it was to the Attorney-General that he applied for reimbursement of the expenses of his trip to London [142].

The columns of Saturday and Monday papers now sounded a fanfare of advertisements for books and pamphlets on the trial and antecedents of Bellingham, hurriedly got together by enterprising journalists. They also reported the funeral of the Prime Minister, whose body, sealed in a lead coffin since Tuesday night, had lain in private state at his Downing Street residence.

On Tuesday morning, the day after his death, Robert Wigram, Member for Fowey, had suggested a public funeral for Perceval, to be attended by all the Members, but Castlereagh vetoed the idea as being unacceptable to the feelings of the family. Brought to full debate at that time, Wigram's suggestion might have resulted in some unhappy and possibly acrimonious argument; it was too soon, only the day after the murder, to raise criticism of the minister while the man still lay on his candle-lit bier. Even the motion of Lord Clive on the following Friday to erect a monument to Perceval in Westminster Abbey – 'the Collegiate Church of Saint Peter Westminster' – was strongly deplored by Opposition members, who were already beginning to stir uncomfortably under the avalanche of laudatory speeches about the deceased minister. 'It was impossible to concur in the vote', declared Whitbread, 'without its having the effect of appearing as an undivided record of the public opinion, on the merits of Mr Perceval's public service.' But though these opposing voices were already being raised, they were not yet strong enough to overcome the mood of mourning. *No, no!* came the overwhelming cry of shocked Members, and the vote for the monument was carried by a majority of a hundred and seventy-three [143].

The funeral itself, then, was to be private, and the wish of the family had been conveyed to the Members of both Houses of Parliament in a circular letter, requesting an avoidance of pageantry and ostentation. But 'so universal was the anxiety to pay all possible respect to Mr Perceval's memory, that this intention was in some measure counteracted.'

The carriages of noblemen and gentlemen had begun assembling in Whitehall opposite Privy Gardens before eight o'clock on Saturday morning, the coachmen and footmen in black and wearing black hatbands. (Cobbett attributed the early hour to a discretion derived from the known unpopularity of the departed Prime Minister.) At nine, a plain hearse drew up at the door of the Downing Street house, and the 'very superb' coffin was placed within. It was inscribed:

Right Honourable Spencer Perceval, Chancellor of the Exchequer, First Lord of the Treasury, Prime Minister of England, Fell by the Hand of an Assassin in the Commons House of Parliament, May 11, A.D. 1812, in the 50th year of his age; born Nov. 1st, A.D. 1762 [144].

The hearse, drawn by six horses and preceded by the plume-bearer, mutes and other attendants, then moved into Whitehall followed by the five mourning coaches – each also drawn by six horses – which had stopped in turn to receive the mourners: Perceval's eldest son, seventeen-year-old Spencer, and his brother Lord Arden, with the latter's chaplain; the Lord Chancellor, the Earls of Liverpool and Harrowby, and Richard Ryder the Home Secretary; Lord Redesdale and other near relatives; the Marquis Wellesley, Lords Sidmouth, Castlereagh, Melville and other great personages, and members of Perceval's confidential staff.

About twenty-one private carriages drew up behind the mourning coaches, and the whole solemn procession moved slowly to the centre of Westminster Bridge, where the black-robed attendants mounted their horses. Silent crowds lined the streets, while the deep tones of the bells of the Abbey and St Margaret's tolled the passing of the murdered man. At Newington Butts, a party of the City Light Horse, of which Perceval had been member and treasurer, fell in to accompany the procession to the little church of St Luke's at Charlton, near Woolwich, where the body would be laid in the family vault. Along the route, shopkeepers respectfully closed their stores.

Meanwhile, the prisoner in Newgate was described as 'composed, and even cheerful, but rather taciturn' on Saturday morning, and made no complaints, though he was refused another request for tea and supplied only with the regulation bread and water allowed to a convicted murderer. He rose a little later than his usual hour of nine o'clock. Newman had considerately arranged to have the cell door left open to extend his walking area, for which Bellingham expressed gratitude.

During the morning, he asked one of the keepers to read a chapter of the New Testament, and listened with rapt attention to the fourth and fifth chapters of St John's First Epistle. He then requested a jelly, as he felt a little faint, but this was refused. Asked by Alderman Matthew Wood, who visited him on Sunday morning, how he found himself, he replied quite cheerfully, ' "As well as a man can be subsisting upon bread and water!" ' but took the opportunity to reiterate his unshaken belief in his innocence of crime. ' "Government think to intimidate me, but they are mistaken, I have been guilty of no offence, having only done an act of public justice" ' [145].

The last two days of his life were kept busy by a variety of visitors to his cell. The sheriff was strict about granting such permission, and many who would have liked to gain admittance, including the Lord Chamberlain, were turned away. Lord Grenville's brother Thomas was quite disgusted by what he called the 'wanton and childish curiosity' that had gripped Lord Hertford. 'He [said] . . . he had just been to Newgate *to see Bellingham*, but that the gaoler had refused to let him see his prisoner. How much better the gaoler knows his duty than the Lord Chamberlain does!' [146]

But others were allowed in, most of them people who were concerned about the state of the prisoner's soul. One of these, intermittently from early Saturday until the fatal last moment, was the prison chaplain, Dr Brownlow Forde, then aged sixty-eight, who – as his duty demanded – paid frequent visits for spiritual advice and consolation. In 1798 Dr Forde, an undistinguished graduate of Trinity College, Dublin, had come from St Catherine's Church in Liverpool to the appointment of Ordinary at Newgate at a salary of £200 plus residence and gratuities. In 1814, a Committee of the House of Commons investigating prison conditions would not be very complimentary about the good doctor's performance of his duties. ('On Sunday, prayers and a sermon in the chapel; on Wednesday and Friday prayers only, without a sermon, in the chapel; on Tuesday and Thursday I attend the condemned prisoners, who also attend in the chapel, if they are of the established church; and when the order comes down for the execution, I attend them regularly every day till that unfortunate event takes place.') But he was ably championed by Basil Montagu, barrister and writer, in a publication the following year, who on his death in 1824 at the age of eighty, after a pensioned retirement, was designated 'a very worthy man . . . much and deservedly esteemed by the City magistrates' [147]. Though he performed his duties punctiliously, he never exceeded them by concerning himself with such problems as sickness and distress outside the exact terms of his contract.

Those convicts sentenced to death for offences other than murder attended the Sunday morning service seated on pews in the middle of the chapel, around a table on which a black coffin was placed. Those convicted of murder were required by law to be kept within their cells, receiving their spiritual comfort from visits by the Ordinary. There was, therefore, no condemned sermon that Sunday, much to the chagrin of the 'numerous visitors of distinction' who, unaware of this fine legal point, had arrived early with the macabre intention of viewing the public behaviour of a man so near his end. An earlier custom, under which the bellman of the parish of nearby St Sepulchre's (who was paid for the service out of a 1612 bequest) went 'into the passage leading to the cells, to pronounce two exhortations to such condemned persons on the solemn night before their execution', had fortunately by now been abolished. 'Their time, it is hoped [would be] much better employed in prayer, and preparation for so awful an event, assisted by some *pious Christians, who frequently come from various parts of the Metropolis, and pray with them the whole of that night,* and until the *Ordinary* arrives in the morning, to attend them in their last moments' [148].

Bellingham, no less than any former occupant of the cell, was to get his share of spiritual advice and exhortation in those last two days.

CHAPTER FIFTEEN

Soon will the hour of mercy be past

AMONG the first of the innumerable applications made to Newman for permission to see Bellingham was that of 'a Scotch Clergyman, of the name of Nicholson', who failed to secure admission. Among those who succeeded was Joseph Butterworth, 'a respectable bookseller of Fleet Street' noted for his piety and said to have been an acquaintance of the prisoner; the Reverend Daniel Wilson, minister of St John's Chapel, Bedford Row (later to become the Bishop of Calcutta); and Perceval's friend James Stephen. All these men were conscientiously and sincerely concerned for the assassin's immortal soul. It may have been under Mr Stephen's wing that Wilson gained access, as the Sunday interview 'took place at the suggestion of a distinguished Member of Parliament, a friend of the late deeply lamented Chancellor of the Exchequer', who had earlier called in to see Bellingham.

The latter 'was calm and rational on Saturday morning,' reported the *Courier* on the 18th, 'as indeed he has been from the first, except when Russia is mentioned, and then he bursts into a violence of manner and language, but by no means either the manner or language of a man of a distempered mind.'

He was very ready to ask God's mercy on his soul and to express contrition for his sins, but he could never be persuaded to count among these the act for which he had been condemned. When the assassination was mentioned, he tended to grow excited, and persisted in justifying his action. This persistence horrified the Reverend Mr Wilson, who reeled from the pages of his *Substance of a Conversation with John Bellingham*, published later in the year, in a perfect frenzy of distress when his earnest exhortations failed to reduce Bellingham to a sobbing penitent [149].

His account of this wrestling with the Devil attracted much attention at the time, though his son-in-law and biographer, the Reverend Josiah Bateman, was not much impressed by it. 'The narrative wants both simplicity and individuality, and can scarcely be considered a happy means of conveying to the public, important scriptural truth,' he wrote piously nearly fifty years later [150]. The Reverend Mr Wilson, however, though he clearly felt he had been bested by the Devil in the encounter, believed the world would benefit by publication of this horrible example.

I ... proceeded to explain to him, as strongly and yet as affectionately as I was able [he recalled shudderingly] the condition of men as sinners before God ... that our transgressions were by far more numerous, as well as more aggravated, than we could possibly conceive, and that ... a genuine abhorrence of sin as committed against Him, were essential to true repentance ...

I then stopped, and said to him, 'I hope I make myself understood.'

'Perfectly,' replied the prisoner: 'I know myself to be a sinner: we come into the world sinners.'

This observation was made in a civil rather than a serious tone, and gave me little hope that he deeply felt the acknowledgment he so readily made.

I then went on to state to him the stupendous love of God to man in giving him a Saviour to deliver him from the wrath to come ... a broken and a contrite heart he will not despise.

I waited with anxiety for his answer. He replied, with a degree of indifference mingled with confidence, without the least shadow of real contrition ... 'I have confessed my sins before God, and I hope in his mercy.'

'This merely cursory acknowledgment of sin,' I replied, 'is totally distinct from true repentance. The heart must be affected, the judgment convinced, the conscience alarmed, and the whole soul filled with sorrow and compunction . . .'

'I confess my sins,' said the unhappy man, in the calm and unfeeling tone which he generally preserved; 'but I cannot say I feel that sorrow you describe, nor that earnest hungering of mind after salvation . . .'

I suddenly stopped the conversation, and, looking him seriously in the face, said, 'I can go on no further . . . Will you permit me, before I proceed, to implore that grace of the Holy Spirit which can alone soften and renew the human mind?'

He complied with great readiness, or rather civility; for his manner was mild, and not at all resembling the ferocity or coarseness of the ruffian; and gave an audible, though tame, assent to most of the petitions I offered, saying, 'Amen,' 'God grant it!' or expressions to that purpose.

When the prayer was finished, I said, 'You see, the object I have been praying for is the very same which I have been endeavouring to urge you to seek; a contrite spirit, a deep apprehension of your totally wrong state of heart . . . O! what will be the misery you will endure, if you rush into his holy presence in an impenitent state! How unspeakably solemn is eternity! Never-ending duration! . . . And how soon,' continued I, my mind gradually adverting to his last most horrid crime, though I did not yet expressly refer to it, 'will this overwhelming scene burst upon you! . . . Every vain excuse, and all your pretensions to repentance, will then vanish . . . Now is the accepted time; now is the day of salvation!'

I am sure every reader will shudder, when I relate, that the prisoner replied to all this, with perfect apathy, 'True, Sir: we none of us know what will take place after death.'

'None of us know!' I exclaimed, almost interrupting him . . . 'This book', I continued, putting my hand upon the Bible which was upon the bench before him, 'reveals a future state of rewards and punishments, the bar of God, heaven and hell, and the grounds of the future judgment . . .'

I now began to be struck with horror at his state of mind. I perceived all too clearly, that though he professed to believe the Bible, he was in fact under the influence of 'an evil heart of unbelief,' which led him to overlook or disregard all the particular truths which the Bible contains. The tranquillity of his manner, and the indifference with which he received what was said, only increased the dejection of my mind. I sat looking upon him for a moment, with astonishment and grief, scarcely knowing how to proceed . . .

I then read to him a letter, stating, that the afflicted Mrs Perceval, with her orphan children, had knelt round the corpse of her murdered husband, and had put up earnest prayers to God for his murderer . . .

As I was standing up to read the letter by a dimly burning candle against the wall of the cell, my friend took particular notice of the murderer's countenance, and distinctly observed . . . he hung down his head for an instant (for he had before been stedfastly looking at us) as though he was much affected. He soon, however, resumed his former attitude, and said, as one recollecting himself, 'This was a Christian spirit! She must be a good woman. Her conduct was more like a Christian's than my own, certainly'. . .

I proceeded as well as I was able to ask him . . . whether he could justify himself to the nation, which he had filled with horror, and consternation, and grief? Could he even excuse to his own conscience an enormity which even heathens held in detestation . . .

He absurdly replied, that he was refused justice.

I had now almost despaired of producing any impression, but I still went on. 'Can your opinion of justice being refused you, warrant your becoming the judge and executioner in your own cause? Was your view of your own case to be considered as infallible? Or, supposing your opinion correct, still can any provocation whatever palliate the foulest and most dreadful of all social enormities, the taking away the life of another? Would you have justified any one who, on the pretence of an affront, should have dared to have planted a dagger in the bosom of your wife or child? . . . Or, supposing you had yourself been in Mr Perceval's situation . . . what should you have thought of a petitioner, merely because he had been disappointed in his application, imagining himself, a private individual, justified in assassinating you, the chief minister of the crown . . . at the very worst, only mistaken in your judgment, whilst in every other act of your life you were exemplary and benevolent?' . . .

The prisoner appeared unable to answer, and I feel persuaded that he was at this juncture, not only convinced of his guilt, but in some degree moved in his obstinate purpose. His eyes were filling with tears. But, unhappily, the few replies he made were, in opposition to the incipient convictions of his mind, of the same character as before . . .

I thought I had exhausted his attention; for his erect position was painful to him, on account of his heavy irons; and said to him, 'Perhaps I weary you too much, by my long conversation.' 'By no means,' he answered, with the mildness which never forsook him: 'What can be more agreeable to me? I should be glad if you could stay with me the whole night'. . . .

'And now,' I proceeded . . . 'let me again and again entreat you to confess and forsake your sins . . . and to spend the few remaining moments of life in escaping from the wrath to come.'

As he made no reply, I went on as well as I was able; for I was by this time almost spent with perturbation of mind and fatigue . . . 'Soon will the hour of mercy be past . . . O, who can conceive the torments of a future state of woe! . . .'

In answer to this he observed, for the third time, and with the same most deplorable apathy, 'I trust in the mercy of God!' . . .

Here the appearance of the keeper of the prison interrupted our conversation. Indeed, it had now continued two hours, and the criminal was evidently exhausted.

So, too, was the Reverend Mr Wilson.

For those periods on Sunday when he was not in conversation with one or other of his visitors, Bellingham walked a little, within the limits imposed by space and his heavy fetters; talked a little with his attendants, often expressing his concern about his family (particularly to the Ordinary, Dr Forde) and wishing he had sent for his wife for a last parting; read the Bible and his prayer book, in which it was observed he had already marked the lessons for that day, which happened to be Whitsunday.

He showed a keen interest in knowing the exact time and place of the execution. The newspapers had begun wondering about the location because of a small difference in the wording of the death sentence, which had pronounced that Bellingham was to be taken not to *the* place, but to *a* place of execution. There was some basis for the rumour that he would be executed on a temporary gallows in Palace Yard, Westminster, near the scene of his crime, as a symbolic gesture of retribution; but to draw to the heart of the country's Government the large crowds expected for the event would have been highly dangerous, and the idea was discarded.

Earl Grey had written to Lord Grenville on the day of the trial:

> I am afraid Bellingham, if he is convicted, of which I do not imagine there can be any doubt, is to be carried from Newgate to Palace Yard for execution on Monday next. I thought it right to state strongly my feeling of the imprudence of such a proceeding, to give it no harsher name, both to the Chancellor and Lord Ellenborough last night in the House of Lords ... The latter was quite violent, said he should recommend it strongly, and indeed was in so heated a state of mind as is quite frightful in a man in his situation. For his own sake, as I have a sincere regard for him, I rejoice that he is not to try Bellingham [*151*].

Thomas Grenville, writing to his brother the Marquis of Buckingham, was even more forthright. 'Hammond, whom I have just met, tells me that Bellingham is convicted, and to be hanged in Palace Yard. If so, our judges are as mad as Bellingham' [*152*].

Towards eleven in the evening, the prisoner received what was probably his last visit, when Joseph Butterworth was admitted. Butterworth, a Coventry man who had been established for more than twenty years as a bookseller at No. 43, Fleet Street, and who, in the following October, would become Member of Parliament for Coventry, was, it seems, known to Bellingham. He was widely known for his philanthropic and charitable endeavours, helped found the British and Foreign Bible Society, and took a special interest in visitors from foreign countries, including Indian chiefs from Canada and Spanish refugees. He held narrow religious views, opposing Catholic Emancipation, but working for many good causes like the abolition of slavery, and was a keen student of the Bible. His conversation with Bellingham was chiefly concerned with his soul, and together they discussed certain verses in

Scripture, 'which [Bellingham] argued on with great zeal. He said, in a few hours more, he should be in a better country than this – for it was a miserable place.'

Even though by now everyone was pretty well assured that he had not been involved in a larger conspiracy, some uncertainty still persisted. Perhaps feeling that he would answer with total truth on the eve of death, Butterworth said he would like to ask one question.

'He said, "I'll tell you any thing you wish to know."

' "Then, had you or had you not, some other person or persons concerned with you in the murder of Mr Perceval?"

' "No: I do most solemnly declare I had not." '

They prayed together until Newman called to escort the visitor out. Bellingham asked for writing materials, which were brought to him. ' "I am going to write a letter to my dear wife" ' [153].

Some accounts of Bellingham's life had declared that relations between husband and wife had been strained to the point of break-up, and that he seldom visited her except to get money. 'A Solicitor was lately employed to draw up articles of separation between him and his wife, but they afterwards made up their difference.' This was later denied; and except for the last five months of his life, when his sojourn in London had a specific purpose, there is no reason to suppose that Bellingham neglected Mary. His obsession, however, had without doubt caused a good deal of discord in the family. It is certainly true, as the *Public Ledger* reported, that Mary had 'for several years maintained herself and family in credit, and occasionally remitted money to her husband. Had not his conduct, previous to his late atrocious act, been eccentric and neglectful, his happiness might have been settled upon a firm basis.' The *Public Ledger*'s concluding comment is less true. 'As it is, he seldom visited her but for the purpose of obtaining the money she had procured, which he spent in pursuit of his chimerical claims upon Government' [154].

He had not been destitute of funds on his return to England – there had been that legacy from Aunt Daw – and his engagement in trading from Liverpool in the Irish commission business after return from Russia brought him some income. Except for the obsession that took him to such a tragic destination, there is no doubt that 'he was a most affectionate husband and father, particularly fond of his children': Mary and his three little boys were the only part of life he was sorry to leave. It had been an enormous comfort to learn that a gentleman from Liverpool had come to town and promised to take an interest in the welfare of his family. Just before midnight, within a few hours of death, writing by the light of the flickering candle, Bellingham penned his last letter to his wife.

My Blessed Mary,

It rejoiced me beyond measure to hear you are likely to be well provided for. I am sure the public at large will participate in, and mitigate your sorrows. I assure you, my love, my sincerest endeavours have ever been directed to your welfare. As we shall not meet any more in this world I sincerely hope we shall do so in the world to come.

My blessing to the boys, with kind remembrance to Miss Stevens, for whom have the greatest regard in consequence of her uniform affection for them. With the purest of intentions it has always been my misfortune to be thwarted, misrepresented, and ill-used in life; but, however, we feel a happy prospect of compensation, in a speedy translation to life eternal. It's not possible to be more calm or placid than I feel, and nine hours more will waft me to those happy shores where bliss is without alloy. Your's, ever affectionate,

JOHN BELLINGHAM

Sunday Night, 11 o'Clock

Dr Ford will forward you my watch, prayer book, with a guinea and note. Once more, God be with you, my sweet Mary. The public sympathise much for me, but I have been called upon to play an anxious card in life [155].

CHAPTER SIXTEEN

The most perfect and awful silence prevailed

VERY early on the morning of Monday, 18 May, the crowds had once again begun to collect around Newgate. Already, in the dim light at four o'clock, windows and rooftops were filling with spectators, many of whom had paid from half-a-crown to two guineas for the privilege. Earlier than that, there had been something for the curious to observe when the workmen began setting up the scaffold, the stage for today's drama [*156*].

> The morning was hazy, thick and wet, heavy showers occasionally falling. The Guards were all in motion at five, and many bodies of military were assembled by six, taking their stations in convenient places least likely to excite public attention.
> The wetness of the morning kept down the extent of the crowd ... At seven ... about two thousand persons were assembled before the Debtors' door of Newgate, around the scaffold of execution; and the Old Bailey seemed to be paved with umbrellas.

The spectators filled Newgate Street: well before eight o'clock the crowd had extended across Holborn into Giltspur Street. The umbrellas were a nuisance, dripping on neighbours and impeding the view. Several were broken as a growl of 'Down with umbrellas!' spread through the mob.

Still fresh in the memories of the populace and the authorities alike was the horrible tragedy of five years earlier at the execution of two murderers, Owen Haggerty and John Holloway, together with Elizabeth Godfrey, when a crowd of about forty thousand gathered to witness the 'turning off'. The pressure became too great: people began pushing and shoving in growing terror. Panic mounted, and when a woman stumbled over a pieman who had bent down to pick up a fallen basket, those behind fell too, and were trampled or suffocated. After the crowd had straggled away, thirty-two persons were found dead; up to a hundred lay screaming and injured.

The police had no wish to see a repetition of this horror. Strong wooden barricades were erected at suitable spots. No carriages were allowed near the scene, to the disgust of carters and waggoners who had expected to reap a harvest from sales of pies and drinks. The scaffold itself, which stood about ten feet above the ground, had extra fences of both wood and iron within which peace-officers with their staves stood to ward off over-eager members of the public. A placard was placed at the entrance to every street leading to Newgate, and placards were also carried about through the streets on poles: *'Beware of entering the Crowd! – Remember Thirty Poor Creatures were pressed to Death by the Crowd when Haggerty and Holloway were executed!'* [157]

Public executions were deplored by many, even then, including the Ordinary, Dr Forde, who had attended all too many, and who only three months later offered his opinion that all executions should take place within the walls of the prison, with nothing more than a black flag displayed and the great bell tolled for public benefit, and the body viewed by none but respited prisoners as a dreadful example. Dr Forde commented to the reformer Basil Montagu:

> Every execution at Newgate, on the present plan, is productive of the worst consequences to the lower orders of the people, as well in the destruction of their little ready cash, as in almost a total subversion of their morals.
>
> The morning of execution is ushered in with one or two

glasses of liquor, on their way to the Old Bailey; where, at seven o'clock at the furthest, they take their places to the amount of from two to four thousand persons (men, women and children) according to the magnitude of the crime, the atrocity with which it has been committed, or the notoriety of the sufferer. In this situation the greater number of the spectators remain . . . for an hour, at least, after the removal of the body; or else chatting with the newly-arriving passengers . . . For this purpose an adjournment is made to their favourite public-houses, wherein they take up their abode, till, from drunkenness or want of money, they are compelled to retire . . . In the mean time their business is neglected, their money expended, their constitutions debilitated, and their families left without support [158].

Inflammatory exhortations – *Rescue Bellingham or die!* – had appeared on walls throughout the town and aggravated a fear of riot. Five thousand troops were quartered near Lamboth in case of need, and other regiments alerted, but the precaution proved unnecessary. The authorities were probably grateful for the poor weather, which seemed to have kept the crowds smaller than they had expected. It was also surmised that uncertainty about where the execution was to take place might have contributed to the smaller turnout. One member of the throng who braved the weather was Lord Byron, who sat up all night to see Bellingham 'launched into eternity' [159].

The dread moment was drawing near. William Cobbett wrote five days later:

While the troops were marching to their stations, while hundreds of special constables, sworn in for the occasion, were flocking to the scene of death; while the carpenters and smiths were, from half-past two o'clock in the morning, disturbing the neighbourhood with their dreadful preparations, he, who was the cause of all this anxiety and turmoil, was sleeping sound in his cell, and 'upon being called between six and seven, said *he was called too soon*' [160].

After writing his last letter to Mary on Sunday night, and adding a note blaming his conviction on Peter Alley's failure to call his long list of witnesses, Bellingham had dozed briefly. Coming out of a short sleep, he handed a shilling to Walker, one of the turnkeys who kept watch in his cell, saying he wished it had been a guinea, and thanking him for his kindness. He then turned over and slept soundly until shortly before six.

Bellingham's behaviour, in fact, during the last moments of his life, drew a curious kind of respect from those who were present. He had said at his trial, ' "If I am destined to sacrifice my life, I shall meet my doom with conscious tranquillity." ' The *Morning Chronicle* would write afterwards: 'Throughout this awful and most impressive scene, his deportment was calm, manly, and even at times dignified; and had he perished for almost any other crime than that of assassination, he would have justly excited the pity and respect, if not the admiration, of everyone who beheld this extraordinary close of his wretched career.'

Had he been truculent, aggressive, they would have been angered; had he shown fear and cringing, they would have despised him. Had he boasted or exulted, he would have antagonized them; had he been vindictive, his spite would have aroused hatred. As it was, the officials and onlookers gave him a confused respect, conversed with him on a level of serious equality, saw him die almost with regret. At this point, his execution had become almost a self-sought privilege, an event that those who were with him had honoured by attending, rather than an event imposed upon him from without.

He had asked and received permission to take the Sacrament this morning in his cell rather than the day before. After he had washed and dressed, he read his prayer book for half an hour, and then, after astonishing Dr Forde by the quality of his extempore prayers, he received the Sacrament. It was noted that he made the responses correctly according to the Church of England, and in a firm voice. When informed that the sheriffs were ready, he replied, ' "I am perfectly ready also", ' and accompanied the Ordinary to the room allotted to condemned prisoners.

At seven, about twenty gentlemen who had been invited to attend had gathered in the Lord Mayor's parlour at the Sessions House. At seven thirty they were joined by the two sheriffs, William Heygate and Samuel Birch, and the deputy sheriff Mr Poynder, shortly followed by the Lord Mayor, all in full-dress suits of black. This group made its way through the underground passages to Newgate, thence through various corridors to the Press Yard, where they stood gathered around, but not too close to, a small anvil in the centre of the yard. Bellingham was immediately brought out. 'He descended into the yard with a firm and intrepid pace, and looking up, he observed, with great coolness – "Ah! It rains heavily".'

A turnkey led him to the anvil on which he was instructed to place his foot for removal of his fetters. Clearly afraid of being hurt, he winced noticeably from the inexperienced hammer blows of the man trying to drive the rivets through the rings: crying, ' "Mind, mind – take care, take care," ' and adding, ' "Strike in the centre, and more firmly, then you will accomplish it." '

He had dressed as carefully as possible for his last appearance, in a round hat, brown greatcoat buttoned halfway up, a blue and buff striped kerseymere waistcoat, clay-coloured pantaloons, white stockings and shoes. One paper noted that these were 'down at the heels', another that he was 'altogether not so neat': not surprising, after his period of imprisonment, and a condition that must have embarrassed him. One of his chief complaints in the condemned cell, where he had not been permitted to shave, had been that he 'could not be able to appear as a Gentleman'.

Fetters removed, he left the yard to return to the room for the condemned, where he was joined by the Lord Mayor and sheriffs and a few others, most of the spectators waiting in an adjoining room. The *Courier* remarked again on his likeness to Burdett, 'much more like . . . than any of the prints make him. He was indeed as like him in his face, in his general appearance and manner altogether, as ever we observed one man like another.' Opposition and 'reformists' were quite enraged by these remarks in Government papers, which they saw as nothing less than an attempt to damage Burdett and his political views by twinning him with an assassin.

The two sheriffs engaged him in a brief conversation, chiefly for reassurance that he had, in truth, been alone in the crime. Heygate was reported to have asked him some searching questions about the state of his soul, and also whether he wanted to pass on any last message. Bellingham explained again that he ' "bore no resentment to Mr Perceval as a man – and as a man I am sorry for his fate . . . It was my own sufferings that caused the melancholy event, and I hope it will be a warning to future Ministers, to attend to the applications and prayers of those who suffer by oppression ... I am sorry for the sufferings I have caused to Mr Perceval's family and friends." ' He added that he hoped Heygate would let the family know of his regret. The sheriff promised to pass on his message, and with real compassion reminded him of the promise that his own family would be taken care of.

He had now changed his shoes for a pair of Hessian boots, and 'turning to the Sheriffs, with a mild but firm tone, said, "Gentlemen, I am quite ready." ' The Ordinary, however, looked at his watch and remarked that ' "we have ten minutes more".'

The elderly executioner, William Brunskill, who had held the position for almost thirty years, and was within two years of retirement, then set to work to bind his hands and pinion his arms, a proceeding Bellingham watched carefully, doing his best to help by turning back his sleeves and clasping his hands together. ' "So?" ' He had examined the rope, which seemed slight to him, and was reassured to be told that it would bear his weight. When his arms were secured by a cord tied behind him, he tested the binding by moving his hands up and down, and asked that it be tightened a little. ' "I wish not to have the power of offering any resistance." ' He also asked that his sleeves be turned down to cover the cords around his wrists.

Brunskill then almost apologetically loosened his cravat in readiness for its removal. ' "Certainly do so." ' said Bellingham, ' "it is perfectly all right".'

It was now time to leave for execution, and the only sign of any break in his composure appeared as he left the room. He was observed to bend his head a little, as though to wipe off a tear on the shoulder of his coat.

The little party now moved quickly to the scaffold. All the prisoners had been locked in their cells, but those in cells opening on to the yards through which Bellingham passed now crowded to the windows to watch him as he went by. He walked with Dr Forde, 'more composed than many of the persons who were present at this awful scene'. The sheriffs and some of the officers preceded, several of the visiting gentlemen followed. The sheriffs, with the Lord Mayor and about six of the visitors, waited on the platform a little below the scaffold in front of the Debtors' Door and covered over from the rain.

> [Bellingham] ascended the scaffold with rather a light step,
> a cheerful countenance, and a confident, a calm, but not at all
> an exulting air; he looked about him a little lightly and
> rapidly, which seems to have been his usual manner and
> gesture; but he had no air of triumph, nor disposition to pay
> attention to the mob, nor did he attempt to address the popu-
> lace . . . [He] submitted quietly, and with a disposition to
> accommodate, in having the rope fastened round his neck,
> nor did he seem to notice any thing whatever that passed in
> the mob, nor was he in any way gratified by the friendly
> disposition which some manifested towards him.

A buzz of voices from some of the mob which had greeted his
appearance had been quickly hushed by cries of 'Silence!' from
the majority.

Had he any last message to send, Dr Forde now asked him, any
final word to say? He started again on the old theme of Russia
and his family, but when reminded that he was on the verge of
stepping into eternity, he stopped at once, and joined the Ordinary
in prayer.

Brunskill was now ready to place over his head the traditional
white cap (more, it seems, to preserve the sensibilities of the onlookers than to blindfold the prisoner, as it was perfectly possible
to see through the thin woven cloth). Bellingham objected to the
cap, but was told it could not be dispensed with.

While it was being tied around the lower part of his face by a
white kerchief, a few people below began calling 'God bless you!
God save you!' Dr Forde asked if he had heard them. He said he
had, but could not make out the words. How did he feel? the
clergyman asked. He thanked God, he said, for having enabled
him to meet his fate with so much fortitude and resignation.

Complete silence had now settled over the scene, and all faces
were turned to the figure on the scaffold. A full minute went by.
The executioner went below to prepare for striking away the sup-
ports, and Forde continued to pray with the prisoner.

> The clock struck eight, and while it was striking the seventh
> time, the Clergyman and Bellingham both fervently praying,
> the supporters of the internal square of the scaffold were
> struck away, and Bellingham dropped out of sight down as

far as his knees, his body being in full view, the Clergyman being left standing on the outer frame of the scaffold. When Bellingham sunk, the most perfect and awful silence prevailed, not even the slightest attempt at a huzza or noise of any kind was made.

CHAPTER SEVENTEEN

I had not the opportunity . . . of publicly refuting those charges

BENEATH the scaffold and out of sight, the executioners were pulling on Bellingham's legs, as they did at most executions, in a merciful attempt to end his sufferings as quickly as possible. Death had probably been instantaneous: he made hardly a movement after the drop. Dr Forde, left standing on the outer part of the scaffold, quickly retired, and in less than ten minutes, most of the mob had begun to move quietly away. Something of Bellingham's own calm had communicated itself to them all.

William Cobbett was one of those who, from his Newgate cell, had witnessed the execution.

The crowd was assembled in the open space, just under the window at which I stood. I saw the anxious looks; I saw the half-horrified countenances; I saw the mournful tears run down; and I heard the unanimous blessings. What, then, were these tears shed, and these blessings bestowed by Englishmen upon *a murderer*! He was a murderer to be sure; the act was unjustifiable; there is no defence to be offered for it without an abandonment of every principle of justice known amongst men; but, the people did not rejoice because a murder had been committed . . . but because his act, clearly wicked as it was in itself, had ridded them of one whom they looked upon as the leader amongst those whom they thought totally bent on the destruction of their liberties [161].

Cobbett, a political animal, saw in the people's reaction a reflection of his own – relief at deliverance from Perceval's policies. But perhaps the mob was responding less knowledgeably, much more simply: giving an uncomplicated and emotional response to a brave man, whatever his crime had been, to one who was unconcerned with presenting an image, who was meeting and accepting death without having given up any of the principles (misguided though they were) that led him to it.

As required by law, the body hung for an hour. When cut down, it was placed in a cart, covered with a sack, and – preceded by the City Marshal on horseback and trailed by a straggling crowd – taken up the Old Bailey, along Newgate Street as far as St-Martin's-le-grand, and round the curve of Little Britain to the house of the beadle of the Company of Surgeons, St Bartholomew's Hospital, in Duke Street. From windows all along the route, faces peered down, and the executioner's boy several times raised the sack to uncover the body for the curious.

The Anatomical Theatre was already crowded with spectators, mostly medical students, when the body arrived for dissection by the eminent surgeon Sir William Blizard. While deploring the 'disgusting spectacle', the papers nevertheless published every gruesome detail; and the *Morning Chronicle* got itself dubbed as gullible for reporting that for five hours after the body was opened, the heart had continued to beat – 'a proof of the steady, undismayed character which he preserved to the last gasp'.

It was reported that 'the great-coat in which he was executed was sold for ten pounds, while other parts of his dress were bought at a price equally exorbitant. The buttons of his clothes were all sold at high prices.' Cobbett interpreted this as a desire to possess relics of a man the populace respected. The Press put it down to morbid sensationalism [162].

On Thursday, 21 May, Sheriff Heygate published a dignified letter denying some of his reported conversation with Bellingham. Perhaps he was sensitive to the implication that he, too, had been probing into the state of the prisoner's soul. The condemned man, he said, had 'earnestly requested the Sheriffs to mention his wife

and family to Government, adding, that as it was a national concern, he thought something would be done for them, and observ-
ing, that he sympathized in the loss which Mr Perceval's family
had experienced; and afterwards said, he should be obliged by my
communicating this circumstance to them.'

Heygate added his own view:

> that [Bellingham] had no accomplice; that his motive . . . was
> an absurd and vague idea of bringing to a public hearing and
> decision . . . his complaints against the Russian Government
> . . . that he entertained no adequate notion of the enormity
> of his crime, having by a singular perversion of judgment,
> formed to himself in a considerable degree, a justification of
> the murder of Mr Perceval, although he reprobated murder
> in the abstract; and that he met death with composure and
> fortitude, but not with eagerness or triumph [163].

It was as fair an assessment as anyone could have made.

Meanwhile, Lord Gower, the villain of Bellingham's piece
(whom, he had said, he would as soon have shot as Perceval) had
been growing restive; he had been denied his day in court when
not called on the day of the trial to answer the charges brought
against him by Bellingham.

He had been loyally supported early on the day of the trial by
his secretary Henry Rick who had rushed to write him an un-
solicited testimonial ('as I supposed it not improbable you may be
called upon to give evidence on the Trial of Bellingham'). Rick
thought it his duty 'to bring to your Lordship's remembrance, that
I have at different times, whilst I had the honor of being with
your Lordship at St Petersburgh, and by your orders given him
small sums of money to support him whilst in prison, and as far
as my recollection goes he never came to your Lordship's house
without being attended by a police officer' [164].

On 17 May, Lord Gower had written an explanatory letter to
Lord Castlereagh, a letter which he asked and received permission
to table in the House of Commons. It was printed in full in the
papers.

> It appears upon the trial of John Bellingham, for the murder
> of Mr Perceval, that the prisoner in his defence endeavoured

to justify that atrocious act on the ground of his Majesty's government having refused to compensate him for the injuries and oppression he states himself to have suffered in Russia, during the time that I had the honour of representing his Majesty in that Country. He complained particularly of my conduct, and that of Sir Stephen Shairpe, his Majesty's consul general, as having sanctioned, by our silence and neglect to interfere in his behalf, the unjust treatment, as he considered it, of the Russian Government.

I was subpoenaed by the prisoner to attend the trial; I did attend, and expected anxiously to be called upon, to state, upon oath, all I could recollect of the circumstances of his case in Russia. In this expectation, however, I was disappointed; my testimony was not called for; and after having heard the most serious accusations of gross neglect of duty and want of common humanity, brought forward by the prisoner, against myself and Sir Stephen Shairpe, I had not the opportunity afforded me of publicly refuting those charges. Although I am perfectly aware that the assertions of a man, standing in the situation of Bellingham, can, unsupported by any other testimony, have no weight whatever with the sober and reflecting part of the public, yet I should be wanting, I think, to the interests and honour of the government of this country, as well as to my own character and reputation, if I did not endeavour to do away any possible misapprehension upon this subject, by as ample a statement of circumstances, as my memory, of transactions which passed some years ago, will allow me to furnish.

In the year 1805, I remember receiving a letter from John Bellingham, complaining of his being detained in prison at Archangel, and claiming my protection, against what he conceived to be the injustice of the constituted authorities of that port; I remember that immediately upon the receipt of this letter, I consulted with Sir Stephen Shairpe, who agreed not only to write a letter to the governor general, requiring an explanation of the circumstances of which Bellingham complained, but also his own mercantile correspondents, British residents at Archangel, for their opinion of the conduct of the Russian government towards the complainant.

It appeared from these inquiries, that Bellingham having

been engaged in commercial business with the house of Dorbecker and Co. pecuniary claims were made by each party against the other, and that these claims had been by the governor general referred for decision to four merchants, two British merchants being appointed on the part of Bellingham, and two other persons on the part of Dorbecker. By the award of those arbitrators, Bellingham was declared to be indebted to the assignees of Dorbecker, the sum of 2,000 rubles. This sum Bellingham, notwithstanding this decision, refused to pay.

It also appeared from the communication received from Archangel, that a criminal suit had been instituted against Bellingham, by owners of a Russian ship which had been lost in the White Sea. They accused him of having written an anonymous letter that had been received by the underwriters in London, in which letter it was stated that the insurance of the ship was a fraudulent transaction; and payment for the loss of her had been in consequence resisted. No satisfactory proof was adduced against Bellingham, and he was acquitted of this charge. But before the termination of this suit, he attempted to quit Archangel, and being stopped by the police, whom he resisted, he was taken to prison; but was soon after liberated, in consequence, I believe, of a second application to the governor from Sir Stephen Shairpe.

About this period I quitted Russia; and I have no recollection of hearing anything more of John Bellingham, till after my arrival at St Petersburgh upon my second embassy. He came running into my house one evening, and solicited me to allow him to remain all night, in order to avoid being retaken into custody by the police, from whom he had escaped. I complied with the request, though I could not, upon any ground, assume to myself the power of protecting him from legal arrest. It appeared that the award of the arbitrators of Archangel had been confirmed by the senate, to which body Bellingham had appealed; and he was in consequence delivered over to the custody of the College of Commerce ... there to remain till he discharged the debt of the 2,000 rubles. This custody was not very strict, for he was allowed to walk wherever he pleased, attended by a police officer belonging to the college. He came frequently to my house, and at various times received from my private secretary small sums of money, to support him during his confinement. Confined as he was by the legal authorities of the country, I could on no pretence make any application for his release; but I remember well, in conversation with the minister for foreign affairs, expressing my personal wish that the Russian government, seeing no prospect of recovering the sum of money required from him, would liberate him from prison, on condition of his immediately returning to England.

Very soon after this conversation, all diplomatic intercourse ceased between the two courts; and the course of public events necessitated my quitting Russia in the abrupt manner with which your lordship is well acquainted. I am, my lord, with great respect, your lordship's most obedient humble servant,

(Signed)   GRANVILLE LEVESON GOWER [165]

The public – or at least that part of it connected with Government and power – was happy to accept Lord Gower's explanations. Cobbett, who was, of course, violently anti-Government, remained dubious, but tried to be fair.

Lord G. L. Gower (*since the death* of Mr Bellingham) has written and caused to be published a letter in vindication of his own conduct and that of the Consul; but, to say nothing of the circumstance of the other party not being alive to answer them, Lord Gower, in stating that Mr Bellingham was imprisoned for the debt of 2,000 rubles, does not say a word about the charge ever having been acknowledged to be a *false* one; and, yet, it is next to impossible not to believe that this was the case. Indeed, this letter of Lord Gower does nothing, in my opinion, either in the way of self-exculpation, or in that of inculpation against Mr Bellingham. The declarations of the two parties are opposed to each other. Mr Bellingham says he was neglected, and abandoned to the scourge of tyranny; Lord Gower says he was not; and, it must be left to the world to judge between them [166].

Perhaps a thread of the same doubt existed in the minds of Andrew Knapp and William Baldwin when they published their

Newgate Calendar some dozen years later. 'We hope, for the honour of our country, that this statement is correct,' though they added, 'and we must confess that a review of all the circumstances tends to confirm its accuracy.' They did, nevertheless, try to be impartial in their judgement.

> As [Bellingham] was grossly misrepresented at the time of his committing the horrid act [they wrote] we think it but justice, revolting as was his turpitude, to state that his widow and friends all bear testimony that his general character was that of strict integrity – a kind husband and father – loyal in his political opinions – and punctual in the observance of religious duties; and the whole tenor of his life, with the exception of the Russian affair, on which it was supposed he was insane, proves him to have been a well-intentioned man [167].

By the time Knapp and Baldwin were writing, many people were having second thoughts that recoiled with horror from the terrible haste with which Bellingham had been hustled through the processes of justice. In less than a week from the time of his criminal act, he had been tried, convicted and hanged.

'He was executed without the least sympathy for his hurried fate, or the slightest public manifestation of feeling that justice in mercy had been withheld from him,' wrote William Townsend, barrister and writer, in 1850. And five years later, Samuel Warren, Queen's Counsel and Recorder of Hull, commented that 'We can with difficulty record calmly that Bellingham's counsel, fortified by strong affidavits of the prisoner's insanity, and that witnesses knowing the fact could be brought from Liverpool and elsewhere, applied in vain for a postponement of the trial' [168].

CHAPTER EIGHTEEN

A very pleasant, affable woman

At the end of the month, advertisements began appearing for a publication entitled *An Appeal to the Generosity of the British Nation, in a Statement of Facts on Behalf of the Afflicted Widow and Unoffending Offspring of the Unfortunate Mr Bellingham*, by George Chalmers, Esq.

Authorship of the *Appeal* was repudiated in various journals, in a letter dated 9 June, by an irate George Chalmers, probably the Scottish antiquary and biographer, of No. 3, James Street, Buckingham Gate ('I cannot any longer be silent ... The Publisher knew ... that he was affixing my name to a Pamphlet that was written by a very different person, with design to do me an injury. I have directed my Solicitor to prosecute ...') [*169*]. But though its author used it as a peg on which to hang an impatient and sarcastic tirade against 'Lord L. Gower and Sir something Shairp' and Perceval's policies in general, the *Appeal* pointed to a feeling of genuine sympathy felt by many people for Bellingham's widow and children.

The dignity with which her husband had faced his tragedy was not wanting in Mary Bellingham too: though still under thirty, she was earning her own right to public respect. She had been harassed by the King's Messengers, who had swooped down in the early hours of the morning to search for Bellingham's papers, by newspaper reporters trying to get interesting snippets of the assassin's domestic life, by civic officials anxious to demonstrate their attention to the causes of political patrons in London. All these people seem to have treated Mary with consideration and interest, and a fair amount of behind-scenes goodwill began to spill itself out in letters and visits and attempts to help; though there were some who feared that support of a murderer's family might be construed as support of murder itself. Had Mary's behaviour at this point shown the least sign of arrogance or complacence, she might have brought down on her head all the fury earlier directed at her husband.

One of her advocates, signing himself 'Anonymous' in a personal letter from Liverpool dated 20 May, presented a compassionate argument to Lord Gower.

[Bellingham's] punishment could not be too ignominious. But, my Lord, that punishment has not been confined to the Villain who was the cause of it, but is extended to his innocent wife and family. His wife, independent of the shock which she must inevitably have received at such an event, is left totally unprovided for, with three helpless children dependent upon her exertions for a livelihood. She has been at once deprived of the support of her husband, and of all the little property she was possessed of, which his expensive residence during five Months in London has squander'd, and at the same time, Her delicate frame has received a blow which totally incapacitates her to attend to her affairs for the present in order to procure immediate subsistence for herself and Family.

'Anonymous' appealed to the conscience of his lordship:

It was only the chance of Fortune which saved you from the Fate of Mr Percival . . . In the Prisoner's explanation of his motives for committing the barbarous deed, he seems most certainly to have been unjustly persecuted, and he imputes some degree of neglect to your Lordship, which, whether false or true, He states to be the remote cause of his unjustifiable conduct. Your Lordship was perhaps the only person living that was aware whether you could have assisted him under his (perhaps supposed) grievances, or whether your services would have been totally unavailable to him. His sense however of the injury He imagined he had unjustly sustained has, it appears, been the origin of his ruin: and possibly now that he has suffered the awful sentence which has hurried him away to a final account, you may now perhaps feel a degree of regret that his application did not meet your more attentive consideration. This, however, is mere conjecture and your Lordship is most probably convinced that every means consistent with your situation was exerted on his behalf, and that ingratitude was the only return for your kindness. Even, however, if this is the case, it is honorable to return *good for evil*.

His lordship was assured by 'Anonymous' that the appeal he now made was totally unknown to Mrs Bellingham:

And I hope that no presentiment that such conduct would be construed by the prisoner's wife into a tacit confession of this imputation of neglect will prevent your lordship's extending the hand of benevolence to alleviate the complicated calamity of the innocent sufferers. No, it would be a confirmation of the general opinion that your duty has been completely fulfilled and that your humane heart was open to the access of calamity even in the offspring of your enemy [170].

To investigate the origin of the letter and the identity of 'Anonymous', Lord Gower turned to his friend and colleague George Canning, who had political connections in Liverpool. Lord Gower seems to have been impressed by the letter – 'It does credit to the writer of it, whoever he may be' – and agreed that any interest he might take in Bellingham's family was 'not likely, or calculated, to subject him to any suspicion of a compunctious acknowledgement of any fault or omission on his part in respect to Bellingham's transactions in Russia; He is perfectly conscious of his blamelessness in this respect.' He therefore asked Canning to pass on to his own colleagues in Liverpool a sum of fifty pounds towards relief for Mary and her children, together with a copy of his own explanation of his conduct as presented to Parliament [171].

Accordingly, John Drinkwater, son of a former mayor of Liverpool, who was assisting Canning's candidacy in the forthcoming election, and his brother-in-law Peter Bourne, son of the current Liverpool mayor John Bourne, together set to work to track down 'Anonymous', and to inquire into the situation of Mary Bellingham.

At nine o'clock on Thursday evening, 28 May, the two men went to Mary's home at No. 46, Duke Street, and were at once shown upstairs to the drawing-room. They were quite impressed by their reception.

'Mrs Bellingham was sitting at the upper end in deep mourning. Her late Husband's Picture was suspended over the chimney piece, & the House altogether appeared to be well furnished.'

After a few moments of small talk, Drinkwater asked if he might read Canning's letter aloud, which would explain the reason for his visit. Miss Stevens came into the room at this point, and both women listened as the letters from Lord Gower and 'Anonymous' were read.

Mary Bellingham 'express'd herself much obliged to her Anonymous friend (whom she has no idea of) & to Lord G. L. Gower for his handsome present'. She commented that her husband's treatment of her showed signs of insanity at times, and that she had decided never to raise the subject of Russia because it so clearly upset him. She also said she had been convinced in conversations with Sir Stephen Shairp (during that dreadful wait in St Petersburg, or later?) that Lord Gower had lacked the authority to interfere in the affair. She 'did all in her power to persuade her Husband of the folly & impropriety of his claims for remuneration from this Government, but all to no purpose, & it is now her greatest consolation to think he must have been insane when he committed the dreadfull act.' She added that she would send a personal letter of thanks to Lord Gower [172].

Having done his duty, Drinkwater reported back to Canning and launched a few of his own opinions. Though he had seemed impressed by Mary and her reception of him, he (and others with whom he had discussed the subject, he said) did not entirely approve of Lord Gower's kindness. 'If he – Lord G – wished to perform some act of benevolence, let him look around him – he will find thousands who have infinitely greater claims than Mrs B.' While he commended Lord Gower's humanity and good intentions, Drinkwater was not too sure about the ultimate effect of 'holding forth to the lower Classes of Society that [Bellingham] has done some meritorious act & that his Children ought to be provided for'.

Any second thoughts he may have had about his temerity in expressing his opinion so freely were dissipated next day, when he picked up Friday's *Liverpool Mercury* – 'a paper remarkable only for its scurrility' – and saw with horror that the fact of Lord Gower's generosity had been made public.

Scurrilous or not (it seemed that the paper's politics were opposed to Drinkwater's), the *Mercury* had printed the information simply as a follow-up to an item in its previous issue. On 22 May, the paper had noted, 'It is with pleasure we hear that a worthy Alderman, with whom we are in the habit of differing widely on political subjects, has generously lent a helping hand to the innocent widow of the criminal and infatuated Bellingham.' Now, on the 29th, its editors were glad to find 'that the example of a worthy Alderman, alluded to in our last number, has been followed by a donation of £50 from Lord G. L. Gower'.

Embarrassed and furious, and sure that none of his relatives who had seen the letter would have divulged the subject to anyone, 'much less to a man of such *Burdett* like principles as him [the editor]', Drinkwater owned he was not surprised when 'On enquiry it prov'd to come from one of [Mrs Bellingham's] intimate acquaintances, a Mr Saunders, like many other of Bellingham's companions, violent unruly Reformists & who are taking all pains imaginable to blazon it forth, to raise subscriptions for her' [*173*].

A tactless move by Mary's father John Neville, in Ireland, dangerously added to the threat of public rejection that might now have built up against her. On 30 May, under the heading 'Subscription for The Widow & Children of Bellingham', the *Freeman's Journal*, Dublin, reported with astonishment an advertisement that had recently appeared in another medium:

St Patrick's Night: a Comic Opera in Two Acts. A subscription is set on foot in England for the Widow of John Bellingham and her three fatherless Children, now left destitute of support; – her Father, willing to contribute his Mite, will Print by Subscription, for their use and benefit, the abovementioned Play, written by him at the close of the Duke of Bedford's Vice-Regency of this Country; revised, corrected, and adapted for the present day. Price 5s. – on

superfine wove Paper 10s. 6d. British. Subscriptions received
by John Neville, in the Commercial Coffee-room; and by all
Booksellers in Town and Country. N.B. The Names of such
Subscribers as wish it, shall be printed with the work.

The *Dublin Journal*, among others, reared up in outraged protest.

That [Bellingham's] family may be much afflicted by the
obloquy which his horrid crime has cast on his name, we can
only conceive; but would this be wiped away by a public
subscription? . . . We are by no means disposed to visit the
crimes of the guilty on their innocent posterity; but it is one
thing not to punish them, and another to reward them for
those crimes . . . Ought a murderer who forfeits his life to the
injured laws of his country to be placed on the same footing
with the warrior? . . .

The editors thought that such a precedent would provide a
kind of bounty on murder. 'Is it come to this, that heroism and
murder are to call forth the same feelings?' The *Dublin Journal*,
while supporting the generosity of any private subscription that
might be set up, saw no reason for a public one [174].

Mary herself took prompt steps to dissociate herself from her
father's gaffe. To English and Irish papers she addressed a repu-
diating letter on 6 June, feeling 'the painful necessity of obtruding
myself into public notice, at a time, and under circumstances,
which make retirement and oblivion of the past peculiarly desir-
able'. Declaring that she had neither solicited nor encouraged a
public subscription, she hoped the proposed publication of *St
Patrick's Night* would not take place, 'and solemnly pledge myself
not to receive any part of the profit that may arise from it'. She
was grateful to friends who had rallied to help; but, she concluded, 'There are other causes of distress, which can only be
alleviated by time, and removed by death' [175].

Uncle James Nevill in Wigan was equally distressed, not only
by the anonymous letter sent to Lord Gower, but by his brother's
poor judgement, 'he being a Man whose conduct has not been
mark'd by prudent care (of which this Marriage was a strong
proof)'. It seems likely that James Nevill disapproved of Mary's

marriage outside the Society of Friends. With sturdy Quaker self-respect, but addressing his lordship with some diffidence – 'a person in thy station of Life to whom I am wholly a stranger' – Uncle James wrote to thank him for his gift to Mary.

He was grateful also, he said, for the humanitarian impulse of John Bridge Aspinall, deputy mayor of Liverpool, and Richard Statham, the town clerk, who had opened a private subscription for his unfortunate niece, with a treasurer appointed to handle donations such as his lordship's. 'This is the third time I have had to provide for her since she became B's wife, first when the Humanity of some English Gentlemen enabl'd her to quit Petersburgh; *great with Child*, she got to my House nearly pennyless, where she lay in.'

After three months with Uncle James, Mary had gone to her father, but his instability created difficulties. Good Uncle James then 'interested myself with her Friends & united in putting her into a little Business, expecting no less than that his (B's) obstinacy would conduct him to Siberia for Life'. He now regretted his advice to Mary to resume life with her husband after his 'Solemn promise to give up wrong thoughts of his wild goose schemes & expectations': but Bellingham had seemed to show his good faith by actually burning some of his papers. 'Had he put the pistol to his own unworthy head, there would have been little cause for lamentation, but alas! the awfull, dreadfull act is done & he suffered the punishment justly due to him' [176].

Mary herself wrote to Lord Gower on 10 June, her concern for her children clearly evident as she found herself

left *totally destitute* with three most interesting, lovely children, all Boys, whose future Welfare and good conduct through life must depend in a great measure upon the education I shall be enabled to give them. To a generous public, I am compelled to look for assistance, now that I am deprived of every other resource, and trust that they will have the liberality to distinguish between the innocent and the guilty. My most ardent *wish* is to *retire* into the Country, there to devote my time and attention to my beloved Children. Compelled by dire necessity I was obliged on my return from Russia, where I left my unfortunate Husband in prison, to exert myself in a line very uncongenial to my feelings, or the

line of life I had been accustomed to move in. Even this has
proved unsuccessful, and I am now deeply involved in the
concern. I hope your Lordship will not deem me impertinent
or presuming on your kindness in thus stating my unhappy
situation, my character upon inquiry I trust would be found a
deserving one, and if thro' your Lordship's interest the great
and wealthy could be induced to contribute to alleviate sufferings almost too great for human nature, I doubt not but the
feelings of their own hearts would be superior to any thanks
I could offer [177].

Among Liverpool residents, Mary had aroused a kind of embarrassed respect. 'Mrs B.'s age is twenty-nine to thirty-one years:
a very pleasant, affable woman: genteel in her manners: rather
short, and was inclined to be lusty, but is now reduced to a
skeleton,' wrote a Liverpudlian to his London friend J. J. Cossart,
who was a Fellow of the Society of Antiquaries and a wine merchant in Clement's Lane, Lombard Street. 'Of his three sons, a
brother-in-law has taken two. You'd be astonished to find how shy
people are of speaking on the subject. Those who have known
him do not like to acknowledge it' [178].

CHAPTER NINETEEN

And in his stead there lives a lazy dolt

LORD GOWER was now garnering his share of the crop of anonymous letters that tend to follow public events.

> Dreadfully are you deceiv'd in thinking Bellingham had no accomplice [wrote a gentleman signing himself 'One of the fifty – Brutus' on 24 May]. Neither shall your pretended Justification in your ignorant letter to the villain Castlereah [*sic*] protect you from the just indignation which is felt at your infamous conduct towards the much injur'd man in Russia. There is many yet must fall, and tho' you think yourself secure, yet before many days are pass'd you'll meet the fate poor Bellingham design'd you. He was my friend from earliest youth and has left a glorious example to the world that a glorious death, after revenge, has nothing frightful in it when compar'd with a life of poverty distress and oppression. Beware the fate which waited Caesar on the ides of March – your fate is decreed therefore prepare for death.

On 25 May, 'A Sincere Espouser of the Cause of Bellingham' penned a note from the Globe Tavern.

From as much as I have read of your Letter addressed to Lord Castlereagh (*that Monster of iniquity & public resentment*) I judge you to be a *mean spirited & cowardly ministerial Fool*. Are not you, my *Lord*, ashamed of publishing such a Letter, when you are well assured that the only person, who could *have any chance* of refuting any part of it (poor Billingham) is long since *Murdered* (as I may say through your & your false & cringing conduct alone). I am at present in haste, but believe me, my *Lord*, you shall hear more of this *cowardly* transaction (e'er long).

In a letter dated 25 July 1818, but most likely to have been written in 1812 (the days of the week coincide with the dates in both years), someone signing himself 'Tim^y Bellingham' challenged his Lordship to a duel. '*I am your man at any weapon* & . . . I will meet you at Primrose Hill on Monday next 27 July at 6 o'clock in the Morning your infamous Conduct towards my lamented friend John Bellingham Esqr has left a stain which nothing can *erase* . . . I am determined to revenge the loss of my friend, his blood calls for vengeance, and as you were the chief in that unfortunate affair, I am resolved to seek your life or loose my own.' In fair play, the writer gave his Lordship warning of his impending doom: 'I shall expect an answer in the Public Ledger on Tuesday.'

Perhaps needless to say, no reply appeared in the columns of the *Public Ledger* either in 1812 or 1818.

Not all the letters were condemnatory. 'A Sincere Lover of His Country' wrote on 19 May to protest a letter published in the *Statesman* which had imputed blame to his Lordship 'as the Cause of Bellingham's having been induced to commit the Atrocious Murder . . . The Absurdity of such an observation is evident to all those who have read the accounts of this man & of his trial.'

And then there was the gentleman of elegant scrolls and flourishes, residing at No. 25, Winchester Row, Paddington, and signing himself 'G. Peacock', who enclosed thirty-two selected and vituperative lines from a 342-line poem entitled 'Bellingham'. His Lordship's Humble & most ob^t Servt had, he said in careful script, been induced to produce a poem in Bellingham's favour, in which unfortunately he had had to speak ill of his Lordship. Nothing would distress him more than to see this poem published, 'on a subject as unpleasant to myself as it can possibly be to you'.

The death of Mr Perceval, who had promised to place the writer in some situation in recognition of his talents, had forced him, he said with regret, into this deplorable act. The distressful state of poverty that had now resulted would make it necessary to publish the work, unless – here was a sample, in advance – his lordship's generosity would enable him to burn it: 'or I shall be obliged to send the manuscript to my employer shortly'.

Overleaf, his astounded lordship was then presented with the judicially chosen extracts from G. Peacock's epic.

> There liv'd in princely pow'r
> A sycophant, a courtier, call'd Lord ——
> It shames the place that gave this reptile birth,
> And shames the man that gave the cypher worth.
> He shames his embassy, & *Sharp* may shame
> Make us forget his base, unmanly name . . .

The reptile does not seem to have been amenable to blackmail. G. Peacock was forced into print in which Bellingham emerged as

> An honest tradesman, of superior sense,
> Bless'd by experience, and by eloquence,
> His credit good, unsullied was his name,
> He paid with pleasure every honest claim.

After this paragon sailed for Russia, G. Peacock's tear-jerking verse continued,

> now began
> Such hardships ne'er before endur'd by man . . .
> Drag'd from his carriage, from a lovely wife,
> Who knew not of his fate, if death or life:
> Drag'd from an infant – his once tender care,
> To loathsome dungeons sent on scanty fare . . .
> 'Adieu!' he cried, 'Mary my love adieu!
> My cause is just, I care not but for you;
> Have courage, here an Englishman is free,
> If there is justice, 'twill be giv'n to me . . .'

But here an Englishman was not to be free. Bellingham would find his troubles only begun.

> 'Twas done – he left her – o'er the pitiless sea,
> Mary was wafted to a country free.
> While he poor man in dungeons spends his hours
> And loathsome food for hunger he devours;
> With malefactors of the blackest cast,
> Is Bellingham the honest Briton class'd,
> March'd through the streets a spectacle of shame,
> Laughed at where he should most protection claim . . .
>
> Still innocence adds courage to his soul,
> And Bellingham is now above controul . . .
> Amidst the threats of exile and of death,
> He breathes a pure, a fearless, dauntless breath,
> Two thousand rubles sets the pris'ner free,
> Which he not owing won't to pay agree . . . .

Free at last and back in England, Bellingham

> hopes to get redress,
> Thinking that Ministers cannot do less;
> Not doubting but an answer will be giv'n,
> (Nor thinking he shall be to madness driv'n.)
> Eight tedious years, and yet no answer made,
> Such base neglect would any one degrade. . . .

Alas, poor Bellingham, lamented G. Peacock.

> To ev'ry office in its turn all round,
> Was Bellingham in quick succession found;
> At ev'ry office was his face well known,
> Familiar by his frequent visits grown.
> E'en those in place were all at last asham'd,
> To hear the man call'd Bellingham e'er named . . .
> Madness succeeds – at intervals alone,
> He swears his base oppressor shall atone . . .
> He waits for G—— determined to fulfil,
> What he conceives a duty – as a will.
> (But hold, beware, as I have said before,

Our hero oft was mad, and here he bore
In looks his madness – tho' his hair ne'er tore.)

Insane through no fault of his own, our hero begins to lie in wait for Lord Gower, but then, deciding 'To let him live and brood o'er former sins,' turns his pistol instead in a different direction.

An hour cuts down
A man that's lov'd, ador'd, in ev'ry town . . .
And in his stead there lives a lazy dolt,
Dull as an ass – and stupid as a colt . . .

In fact, his lordship, recognizable equally as reptile or jackass. Bellingham, however, is made of nobler clay.

Yet let a tear of pity wet his grave,
A man in honour nice, in spirit brave:
Superior dignity – intrinsic worth,
Unsullied character and honest birth;
Fair in each action, till the last sad day,
Which fill'd us with alarm and dire dismay.
He pitied him whose death we all lament,
Own'd 'twas revenge on G—— that he meant;
Paid tribute to the virtues of the dead,
Honour'd the man whose noble spirit's fled;
Pray'd that his wife and children might be fed
Nor know to want a friend – is want of breath,
Ask'd noble minds to let his sons be taught,
What by experience he dearly bought [179].

With this epic (at least it scanned) G. Peacock hardly leaped to the forefront of English poetic tradition, and Bellingham failed to become a folk hero. Yet though Mr Peacock's bad verse scarcely inspires, it carries its tiny grain of truth. Those who have since had time to think about the event have been forced to sober and uncomfortable comment on the treatment accorded a man whose sufferings had gone beyond what his mind was capable of bearing.

Then there were the *curiosa*, the oddities snapped up to enliven the columns of the daily journals. Nothing, it seemed, was too remote to be dragged in, if the slightest thread of relevance could be found to tie it to the assassination.

Old Moore's Almanack, for instance, had predicted dire happenings for 1812. Pointing out the unfavourable position of the planets at the end of the spring quarter, Old Moore had looked into the future and seen the possibility 'that their opposition may tend to frustrate the ablest designs for the public service, if not hasten the death of some great man'.

One true coincidence was noted – the death of William Pitt, Earl of Chatham, on 11 May 1778. Several journals recalled that an ancestor of Mr Perceval had been the victim of assassination in 1657. There was, moreover, an earlier John Bellingham, equally villainous, who had been hanged in 1709 for forgery. And anyone who turned the pages of the current Law List would find a remarkable juxtaposition: the name of Perceval, immediately followed by the name of Bellingham, where Spencer Perceval was listed as Chancellor of the Exchequer, and immediately above appeared the name of the Secretary, Sir George Bellingham [180].

There were also the rumours and the crop of precognizant dreams. A man had started back (in Hull, in London, in Liverpool) on hearing of the murder, and cried out, ' "If 'tis so, 'tis Bellingham who has done it!" ' Someone in Dumfries, it was said, had circulated the fact of Perceval's death twenty-four hours before the event. This was later proved to have been unfounded ('Who doubted it?' sniffed the *Newcastle Journal*); it referred to the murder of a manufacturer in a rioting northern town [181].

The most authentic and seemingly inexplicable instance of precognition was the dream experienced by a reputable gentleman in Cornwall, some nine or ten days before the assassination. John Williams, of Scorrier House, Redruth, a banker and mining engineer of the utmost respectability, had a vivid dream in which he found himself standing in the lobby of the House of Commons.

A small man, dressed in a blue coat and white waistcoat, entered; and immediately I saw a person, whom I had observed on my first entrance, dressed in a snuff-coloured coat and yellow metal buttons, take a pistol from under his coat and present it at the little man above mentioned.

The pistol was discharged, and the ball entered under the left breast of the person at whom it was directed. I saw the

blood issue from the place where the ball had struck him; his
countenance instantly altered, and he fell to the ground.
Upon inquiry who the sufferer might be, I was informed that
he was the Chancellor. I understood him to be Mr Perceval,
who was Chancellor of the Exchequer. I further saw the
murderer laid hold of by several of the gentlemen in the room
[182].

At this point, Mr Williams awakened, and told the dream to his
wife, who hushed him with the assurance that it was only a dream,
and he went back to sleep. At once the same dream played itself
out again in his mind; his wife again showing scepticism, he fell
asleep a third time, only to go through the whole scene as before.

In considerable agitation, he began to wonder if he ought to go
to London to warn the Chancellor. Next day he related the dream
to some business acquaintances at a mine in the neighbourhood,
and asked for their advice. They felt, however, that the journey he
contemplated might lay him open to ridicule as a fanatic. He said
no more, but watched the papers with close attention.

On the evening of 13 May, one of his sons, returning from a visit
to Truro, rushed into his room crying, ' "Father, your dream has
come true! Mr Perceval has been shot in the lobby of the House
of Commons!" '

Not long afterwards, Mr Williams had occasion to visit London.

And in one of the print-shops [I] saw a drawing for sale
representing the place and circumstances which attended Mr
Perceval's death. I purchased it; and, upon a careful examination, I found it to coincide in all particulars with the scene
which had passed through my imagination in my dreams. The
colours of the dresses, the buttons of the assassin's coat, the
white waistcoat of Mr Perceval, the spot of blood upon it, and
the countenance and the attitude of all those present, were
exactly what I had dreamed.

The details of the dream made such an impression on all who
heard them that Williams was eventually asked to meet two
officials from the Admiralty in the home of John Rennie, the civil
engineer who designed the Southwark, London and Waterloo
Bridges. Here he related his dream once again, 'and all present

believed him'. Both Williams and Rennie were men of sufficient repute to take their place in the pages of *The Dictionary of National Biography*. In 1838, Williams dictated an account in his own words, which was signed and attested by witnesses.

Perceval himself seems to have had some premonition of death, though perhaps it was induced by thoughts about his will, which he had drawn up about four years earlier, but of which he had only recently, at the beginning of April 1812, handed a copy to his wife. Mr Matthew Montague, who later succeeded to the title of Lord Rokeby, remembered afterwards that Perceval had felt 'strong apprehensions of his impending fate for several days before it took place, and that he had given his will to Mrs Perceval, with some expressions indicating its probability' [*183*].

CHAPTER TWENTY

Something like compassion

JUST over thirty years later, another assassin, trying to kill another Prime Minister of Britain, succeeded in murdering his secretary instead; but, apprehended, met with a fate more civilized than was meted out to John Bellingham.

On 20 January 1843, at Charing Cross, a young Glasgow turner, thirty-year-old Daniel MacNaghten, shot and killed Edward Drummond, secretary to Sir Robert Peel, in the apparent belief that he was killing the Prime Minister himself. (By one of those stranger-than-fiction coincidences, this victim of assassination, too, was buried in the little church at Charlton where Perceval's body had lain since 1812.)

At his trial, it became clear that MacNaghten was far from sane. He thought he was being followed by 'a parcel of devils', from whom he could not escape even when he fled to France. No sooner had he landed at Boulogne, he said, than 'he saw one of his spies peep from behind' the watch-box on the quay. 'The Tories had joined with the Catholics' in persecuting him [*184*].

The assassination shocked Britain just as the earlier one had done, and public opinion was roused against MacNaghten almost as vindictively as it had been against Bellingham; except, of course, that this tragedy did not so dangerously threaten the ship of state. But in the intervening years the law restricting certain of the prisoner's rights to counsel had changed. MacNaghten's counsel, Alexander Cockburn, Q.C. (later Lord Chief Justice of England), offered a masterly defence that won a verdict of 'not guilty on the ground of insanity'. In fact, his arguments were so persuasive that the Lord Chief Justice, Nicholas Tindal, interrupted to ask whether the Solicitor-General had evidence that could combat the medical testimony – ' "because we think, if you have not, we must be under the necessity of stopping the case" '.

The Solicitor-General had not, and the jury returned the verdict without retiring.

Out of this trial came what are known as the 'MacNaghten Rules', on which, in most English-speaking jurisdictions, the insanity concept in criminal law is based today. Following public outcry against the verdict, the House of Lords presented five questions to the judges of England. Though the answers they returned have been open to widely differing interpretations, they are still generally accepted as authoritative. Had the MacNaghten Rules been in effect at Bellingham's trial, he must have been judged insane on the answer to the second question 'that undoubted evidence ought to be adduced that the accused was of diseased mind, and that at the time he committed the act he was not conscious of right or wrong' [185].

Inevitably, comparisons were made at the time. In 1835, the eminent physician Dr James Cowles Prichard had noted, 'I believe that few persons now entertain doubt of Bellingham's insanity' [186]. Cockburn, defending MacNaghten, recalled the fate of the earlier assassin.

'Gentlemen, it is a fact that Bellingham was hanged within one week after the commission of the fatal act, while persons were on their way to England who had known him for years, and who were prepared to give decisive evidence of his insanity. He was tried – he was executed, notwithstanding the earnest appeal of Mr Alley, his counsel, that time might be afforded him to obtain evidence as to the nature and extent of the malady to which Bellingham was subject.'

After giving other examples of insanity, Cockburn summed up

'the practical conclusion of these investigations of modern science upon the subject of insanity. It is simply this – that a man, though his mind may be sane upon other points, may, by the effect of mental disease, be rendered wholly incompetent to see some one or more of the relations of subsisting things around him in their true light, and though possessed of moral perception and control in general, may become the creature and the victim of some impulse so irresistibly strong as to annihilate all possibility of self dominion or resistance in the particular instance; and this being so, it follows, that if, under such an impulse, a man commits an act which the law denounces and visits with punishment, he cannot be made subject to such punishment, because he is not under the restraint of those motives which could alone create human responsibility' [187].

The victory of commonsense, justice and mercy in MacNaghten's case was a legal victory, not a popular one. 'It is feared he will get off on the plea of madness,' wrote Thomas Raikes in his diary on 28 January, 'in which case, no man's life will be safe' [188]. Public indignation was as vociferous against MacNaghten as it had been against Bellingham, and his execution would have been welcomed with the same general approval and sense of justice felt by the majority of those who, in 1812, considered themselves to be right-thinking, law-abiding citizens. But Bellingham's fate carries overtones of lynch law – the submission to the hot fury of the moment that blots out reason and justice and in itself is a form of mass insanity.

Revenge, had this been Bellingham's motive, might have been better understood, and execution a proper and natural consequence in terms of the day's laws, though nothing could forgive the vindictive haste with which Bellingham was hustled to this consequence. Getting even could be comprehended by nearly everyone – nearly everyone having at some time or other been gripped by the unreasoning need to absolve bitterness by a tit-for-tat. Even carried to the ultimate excess of murder, revenge would have been regarded not as insanity, but as the most extreme behaviour of normality, though the souring hatreds that drive a person into narrowing channels of futility may easily turn to monomania. What bothered later critics was less what they saw as the proper justice exacted for revenge, than the horrible fear that,

if it were not revenge but insanity, justice in this instance had
failed.

There remain discrepancies in the case, for want of access to
papers that may be unavailable, or may have vanished. Though
the lack of these does not in any way dispute the fact of Bellingham's obvious insanity, a few small unsatisfied questions remain
to nag at the edge of the mind.

What happened, for instance, to the original debt of 4,890
roubles about which all Bellingham's early petitions were concerned? Specifically, 4,890.88 roubles, so precise were some of his
statements. Where did the later figure of 2,000 roubles – the only
figure mentioned in 1812 – spring from? And why, if clear evidence existed to the contrary, did he insist, while he was still firmly
held in the grip of those who could bring dire punishment down
on his head, that one of the arbitrators had changed the verdict
given earlier under oath? If Bellingham, once freed, went so far
as to impeach the Governor-General of Archangel for a false oath,
this alone, if without foundation, should surely have been the
strongest possible evidence of the insanity the Government refused to admit at his trial.

Later generations may deplore the fate of a man clearly insane
who met instead the fate of a criminal. Bellingham, seeing himself
sane, did not. In fact, his removal to a place of confinement for
the insane might well have been a punishment more cruel and
pitiless than death. By the justice of his act, as he saw it, he had
achieved his redress. By this act he had righted the wrongs he had
suffered, and by bringing his quest to one irreversible end, he
had arrived at peace of mind. One can imagine, with horror, the
anguish of such a mind forced to recognize that his idea of justice
was regarded as insanity, that his peace could be nothing more
than a treadmill of inescapable memories.

What kind of a man was he, in truth? An inadequate man, probably, who desperately needed to be assured of adequacy; a man
to whom failure was an affront, that made him an object of ridicule to others, a man who could not accept the presence in himself
of any weakness. Obstinacy was his expression of strength; he took
contradiction as an insult to his intelligence. This was a man whose
streak of madness might have remained safely buried if it had
not been surfaced by the stresses of misfortune.

He was 'a pleasant and inoffensive companion, but when he had disputed accounts in business, which was often the case, he then shewed his obstinate and unyielding disposition'. When his wife was told of his fearful deed, she exclaimed (or was reported to have exclaimed), 'I do not wonder at it, for his vindictive temper he never could restrain' [189]. But he was not known as a violent man except in terms of his vehemence whenever the Russian fiasco was discussed. Small successes were probably all he needed, but he met instead tremendous failures. Acts of God he might have had the courage to bear with humility and dignity: failures rooted in personal incompetence he could not face.

'Bellingham had very little acquaintance at this place, and was indeed very little known, as his business was not of much magnitude,' wrote J. J. Cossart's friend from Liverpool. 'He did some little to Russia: but, since the disturbance with that country, turned his attention to the Irish Commission Business' [190].

His trade was small, and he was inclined to be reserved. He was not, for instance, a member of The Lyceum, where merchants and shipowners sat comfortably in the big news room, sipping coffee; they watched the dial, set high in the wall, that recorded the direction of the weathervane on the roof and told them when the wind had changed, so that they might go down to the quay and await the imminent arrival of long-looked-for ships. 'The assassin had been a resident here for about three years; and his principal business was purchasing iron for the Irish Market,' wrote another Liverpool merchant to a friend in Perth. 'He was not generally known, and although I must have spoken to him more than once, I do not recollect him' [191].

He was not wildly ambitious, nor was he a gregarious man with any need to be dominant in a group. He does not seem to have belonged to the breed that gathers in jovial companionship with others of the same trade or profession in clubs or societies. He remained an outsider, a solitary operator, warm in his private relationships, aloof with acquaintances, a touchy personality who might have been able to rationalize a private failure, but could not face a public degradation that paraded him as inept, dishonest and helpless. His behaviour during detention, trial and execution hardly mirrors the image of the turbulent, irritable, aggressive, loud-mouthed person that the events attributed to him in early life and in Russia seem to project. The man who on one notable occasion behaved 'indecorously' in Archangel may have had reason for bursting so uncharacteristically from the smooth shell of dignity he presented to the world. It was so far from his normal behaviour as to have been worthy of remark at the time, and his frequent aggrieved references to this one outburst seem to show how it rankled in his mind. Betrayal into such a loss of control, for Bellingham, would be a sign of weakness that he could not easily forget or forgive in himself, nor could he forgive those whose actions had caused him thus to lose face.

Reflecting the contemporary opinion that punishment for crime must be severe, the *Quarterly Review* could yet allow a note of pity for this criminal. 'For that unhappy man, though never was the forfeiture of life more imperiously required for the sake of society, it was impossible not to feel something like compassion' [*192*].

'We shall forbear, at present, making any comments on the character and conduct of a man whom we must consider insane,' said the *Liverpool Mercury* at the end of May, 'although it appears he has . . . been considerably misrepresented, as we hear from very good authority, that the alleged separation from his wife was wholly unfounded; and that he was always remarkably solicitous about the welfare of his family . . .' [*193*]

'He was a most affectionate husband and father, particularly fond of his children (three boys), the eldest about nine years of age, the youngest about eleven months,' J. J. Cossart had been told. And, 'In his manners he was kind to his Family,' wrote Mary's Uncle James sorrowfully, 'but in his conduct uniformly cruel' [*194*].

Mary struggled on alone, except for Miss Stevens, with her millinery business. By the end of the year, she was ready to give up the struggle. On the front page of the *Liverpool Mercury* for 13 November, she placed a sad and defeated advertisement:

M. Bellingham presents her best respects and sincere thanks to the Ladies of Liverpool and its Environs, who have favoured her and her Partner, Miss Stevens, with their Orders; she is sorry to inform them that she has been reduced, by unprecedented misfortunes and distress, to the necessity of compounding with her Creditors for ten shillings in the pound, in order to pay which, she is obliged to offer her

Millinery, Dresses, &c &c which she has selected in London for this Season, with her Whole Stock in Trade, at Cost Price, for Ready Money. On Tuesday next, the 17th, she opens her Rooms for this purpose, when she most earnestly solicits the attendance of her Friends and the Public. At the same time requesting the liquidation of all debts due to the firm of Bellingham and Stevens – with the most painful sensations she feels the necessity of adopting this measure, having no other means of supporting herself and three Fatherless Children than what may arise from her present line of Business. 46 Duke Street.

Writing to George Canning after his interview with Mary, John Drinkwater had noted: 'It is her intention to take the name of Nevill.' A Mary Nevill was living at No. 14 Seymour Street in 1818, at No. 71 Islington Street in 1821 [195]. Thereafter she disappears, and her three little boys with her. It would be pleasant to know that they grew up and did well, the tragedy of their childhood dimmed by time. If, as seems likely, the Henry Stevens Neville who died in London in 1875, childless but prosperous, and who had married a granddaughter of old James Nevill of Wigan, was the baby Henry about whom John Bellingham was so concerned in 1812, it is pleasant to realize that he could successfully survive so unhappy a background. With persistence they could be precisely traced; but they might, perhaps, prefer to vanish from the pages of history.

The other bereaved wife, Jane Perceval, bore her loss with courage, though with none of the privations with which Mary had to cope. It was said by the *Public Ledger* and other papers that she had gathered her family around her at the moment of Bellingham's execution to pray forgiveness for the soul of her husband's murderer. 'Mrs Perceval though exquisitely & deeply sensible of the Loss she has sustained, has with the most becoming fortitude composed her mind to meet the situation in which it has placed her, & . . . she is in an exemplary manner exerting herself in the Discharge of its Duties,' wrote Perceval's brother Lord Arden on 30 July to the Lord Bishop of Bristol [196]. In January 1815 she took as a second husband Lieutenant-Colonel Sir Henry Carr, and lived with him happily until his death in August 1821. She died in January 1844, aged seventy-four.

The business of the nation continued, limping a bit, it is true, in the almost total confusion that had followed the tragedy. A writ had been moved in the House of Commons on 20 May for the election of a new Member for Northampton in place of Perceval, and the electors of the borough held a meeting in the Northampton Guildhall to consider asking Lord Compton, son of his cousin the Earl of Northampton, to accept the nomination (he was elected in October). On 5 June the Corporation voted £105 towards the erection of a monument to Perceval's memory in All Saints' Church, which, after his death, had been hung with sombre black. The Government struck a medal to commemorate the assassination, bearing a likeness of the slain Prime Minister on one side; on the other, Great Britain was portrayed pointing mournfully to a broken column as a sad symbol of the nation's loss.

Henry Brougham allowed no halt to his assault on the Orders in Council, and petitions continued to be heard both for and against repeal. Even while ministers and Members were still floundering, only two days after the assassination, witnesses who had come to town to appear before the Committee were beginning to mutter 'that they suffer great inconvenience being absent from their respective concerns', adding virtuously that though 'they cannot refrain from expressing their regret and abhorrence at the melancholy and atrocious event which has suspended the course of public business', they were 'less induced by personal motives than by the sense which they entertain of the great importance to the Country of their examination being proceeded in' [197].

On 23 June, the Orders in Council restricting trade with the United States were at last repealed. Only five days earlier, on the 18th, a formal declaration of war against Britain had been made by the American Congress at Washington.

The old Government at Westminster was still in power, with most of the old policies, under Lord Liverpool, who (appointed 8 June) now began a term as Prime Minister that would last until 1827. A more candid view of Perceval began to present itself, once the compassion for the man had ceased to obscure the assessment of the minister, though political attitudes still coloured the judgements of the assessors.

All except fanatical opponents granted him his virtues. 'A man of unblemished character in private life; mild, benevolent, religious, and uniformly correct in all his conduct ... He was a very acute debater ... his temper was good; and he never lost sight of the spirit, or manners of a gentleman; nor carried his hostility beyond the walls of the House of Commons' [198].

From this base of agreement, his critics shot off at varying tangents. The *Edinburgh Review* qualified its concessions with savage buts:

> With every private virtue, however, which could adorn a human being, he was unquestionable the most mischievous of all the bad ministers who, for these thirty years past, have been placed at the head of affairs, in this country ... As a minister of finance, he was profuse, and deficient of vigour ... He seemed to suppose, that rectitude of intention was alone a sufficient reason for self-confidence; and therefore feared nothing because he meant well ...

In the view of the *Monthly Magazine*, 'since the Revolution England has not had a more incapable and unpopular minister, than this unfortunate gentleman'; deploring 'his fatal errors as a politician ... the intrigues by which he obtained and retained his office ... his narrow and illiberal views on all subjects, domestic and foreign ... his bigotry on all points of religious toleration; and ... his total want of address and management' [199].

He had his admirers and adherents, who mourned him as 'a man of rare abilities ... his politics were in progression with the great destinies of his country, and his liberality kept pace with the march of the times; he presented the single instance of a great statesman formed out of the practised lawyer'. Queen Charlotte only hoped the Prince Regent would be lucky enough to find in his successor 'equal talents & integrity'. The *Courier* had the settled faith 'that at no period of her history did Great Britain possess a First Minister more adapted to the existing circumstances of his country' [200].

It seems curious, reading today of his fluency in debate and brilliance in prosecution, and the vigour of his participation in politics, that the pall of obscurity has so thoroughly shadowed Perceval's place in history.

In 1887, when the latest volume of the great new *Dictionary of National Biography* came out, the inevitable critics fired the in-

evitable broadsides against the inclusions and exclusions, though
more often against the exclusions, for which they had their own
candidates. In the July 1887 issue of *Notes and Queries*, Mr
Edward R. Vyvyan protested the failure to include Bellingham
among the famous, as 'a man celebrated by his infamy'. Up to this
point in the *Dictionary*, the entry coming nearest to infamy had
been that of Eugene Aram, concisely defined as 'criminal'.

A few correspondents recoiled from the idea of thus seeming to
approve wickedness and depravity by publicity. If such as Bel
lingham were to be included, asked the scholar Edward Watford,
'Where is the line to be drawn, and why should not a place be
found for Burke and Thurtell, Greenacre and Tawell, and "Mr"
Peace?'

But the consensus supported the proposition that Bellingham
should have been included. 'If life produces "horrors", the "horrors" ought to appear in a large book that professes to give a
history of life in a copious series of biographies . . . We have
nothing to do with good and bad in biography; notoriety is the
point . . . Notoriety is far from propriety; but history and biography are concerned with notorieties.'

Perhaps the editors took note. Burke is there, and Thurtell and
Greenacre (but not Tawell or Peace). Second thoughts came too
late for Bellingham's inclusion, though it was well argued that he
should not be compared with ordinary murderers because his
crime had 'exalted him into an historical personage'. After all, a
similar act has kept alive the name of Charlotte Corday.

But it was a false prophet who wrote in *Notes and Queries* that
'[Bellingham's] name will always be remembered by every English
schoolboy' [201]. Posterity has almost forgotten both victim and
assassin. Few people, other than historians, recognize the name of
Spencer Perceval today, and there is hardly anyone who knows
(many are frankly sceptical) that the nation was, in truth, once
rocked when a British Prime Minister fell by the hand of an
assassin.

Notes

Full titles of sources given below will be found in the Bibliography, listed alphabetically under abbreviated form.

1. The account of the assassination and the events of the next few days has made use of the following sources, as well as those specifically attributed: *The Times; Morning Chronicle; Morning Post; Courier; Sun; Liverpool Mercury; Northampton Mercury; Nottingham Journal; National Adviser; European Magazine; Political Register;* Cobbett; Jerdan; Authentic Account; *Annual Register*, 1812; *Public Ledger*; Forbes.
2. *European Magazine*, p. 373.
3. Cobbett, para. 127.
4. B.M., Add. MSS. 29,764.
5. Fisher, vol. 1, p. 7.
6. Ibid., p. 6.
7. Holland, Book II, p. 129.
8. *Courier*, 12 May 1812; Forbes, p. 8.
9. Bath Archives, vol. 1, p. 374.
10. Romilly, vol. 2, p. 256.
11. Malmesbury, vol. 2, p. 275.
12. Jerdan, vol. 1, p. 140.
13. Farington, vol. 7, p. 83.
14. Jerningham, vol. 2, p. 20.
15. Aspinall, vol. 1, p. 74; *Courier*, 13 May.
16. Berry, vol. 2, p. 497.
17. Calvert, p. 184.
18. Perceval (Holland) Papers.
19. B.M. Add. MSS., Perceval Papers, 12 May 1812.
20. G.L.R.O./O.B./S.R./13 May 1812.
21. *Morning Chronicle*, 13 and 18 May.
22. Colchester, vol. 2, p. 380.
23. Robert Plumer Ward, vol. 1, p. 476; *Morning Chronicle*, 15 May; *The Times.*
24. *Courier*, 27 May.
25. Eldon, vol. 2, p. 203.

26. Bath Archives, vol. 1, p. 375.
27. *The Times*, 1 June.
28. *Morning Chronicle*, 14 May.
29. Ibid.
30. *Morning Chronicle*, 14 May; Colquhoun, p. 227.
31. B.M. Add. MSS. 49,195.
32. Chalmers, p. 19: *Examiner*, 17 May.
33. *Courier*, 14 May.
34. Hassall, p. 190.
35. *Lincoln's Inn*, vol. 4, pp. 124–7; B.M. Add. MSS. 38,251.
36. *Northampton Mercury*, 23 May, 6 June; *Morning Post*, 20 May; *Morning Chronicle*, 23 May.
37. Northampton Records, vol. 2, p. 487; *Nottingham Journal*, 6 June; *Public Ledger*, 13 May.
38. *Courier*, 18 May; *Morning Chronicle*, 25 May; *The Times*, 23 May.
39. *Morning Chronicle*, 13 May.
40. *Courier*, 15 May.
41. Calvert, pp. 184, 185.
42. Bessborough, p. 222; *Morning Chronicle*, 20 May.
43. *Morning Chronicle*, 16 and 20 May.
44. *Liverpool Mercury*, 26 June; *National Adviser*, 27 June.
45. *Annual Register*, 1812 (General History), p. 70.
46. *Courier*, 13 May.
47. Calvert, p. 186.
48. *Edinburgh Weekly Journal*, 9 June.
49. Ward, John, p. 156. 'Ivy' was Helen D'Arcy Stewart (Mrs Dugald Stewart), third daughter of the Hon. George Cranstoun.
50. B.M. Add. MSS. 48,216; P.R.O. 30/29/6/11.
51. *European Magazine* (1812), vol. 61, p. 367.
52. *Courier*, 14 May.
53. *Morning Chronicle*, 15 May.
54. *Courier*, 14 and 15 May; Holden's Directory, 1811.
55. *The Times*, 18 May.
56. *European Magazine* (1812), vol. 61, pp. 368–9.
57. Wilson, p. 32.
58. Graves, p. 31; Guildhall Library MSS 10354/2; St-Dunstan-in-the-West parish registers.
59. Information about Bellingham's family may be found in the following sources: Wilson; Brooke; relevant parish registers (St Neots, Huntingdon Bishop's Transcripts, St-Dunstan-in-the-West, St George's, Hanover Square); Rate Books, St Marylebone.
60. Wilson, p. 32.
61. New Complete Guide, 1783; Wakefield's Directory, 1794.
62. Brooke, p. 480; Wilson, p. 32.
63. Information about *Hartwell* comes from I.O.R. L/MAR/B 461A, B100, B101, B103, B105, B106; *The Times*, 24 April, 13, 17, 21, 24 and 27 August 1787; *Gentleman's Magazine*, 1787, pt. 2, p. 735.
64. Wakefield's Directory, 1794; Wilson, p. 34; Brooke, p. 480.

65. Wilson, p. 34; Brooke, p. 480; Smith, W.; *The Times*, 10 March 1794; *Morning Chronicle*, 7 November 1796; *Morning Post*, 5 January 1795 and 29 March 1799.

66. *Full Report*, p. 53.

67. *Hull Advertiser*, 31 January 1801; December 1800 – December 1801 and later years.

68. Peck, *Hull Advertiser*, 23 May 1812.

69. Crossle MSS., vol. 7, p. 247; vol. 22, pp. 15, 32–3, 72, 107, 243, 253, 259, 261, 335. In some sources Mary was named Mary Ann.

70. *British Factory*, p. 31; Parker, pp. 177, 179.

71. Cobbett, para. 127.

72. *Macbeth*, III, 1.

73. Lloyd's List, 1803.

74. This account of Bellingham's experiences in Russia is based on B.M. Add. MSS. 48,216 and P.R.O. 30/29/6/11, with some details from Old Bailey Sessions Papers, 1812. Some information about the firm of R. Van Brienen appears in an advertisement in *The Times*, 4 July 1804; Vassiley Popoff is listed in *Russkiy biograficheskii slovar*.

75. Storch, p. 139.

76. Carr, p. 218.

77. *Hull Advertiser*, 16 May 1812.

78. Clarke, vol. 1, p. 7.

79. Zacek, p. 201; Grellet, vol. 1, pp. 392–3, 406.

80. *Full Report*, p. 52.

81. Information about James Nevill may be found in Society of Friends Quarterly Meeting of Lancashire burials 1654–1838; marriages 1652–1837; births 1645–1837; Lancashire Record Office, James Nevill, 29 April 1852; P.R.O. 30/29/6/11.

82. Jackson, vol. 2, p. 121 (17 June 1807).

83. *Full Report*, p. 52.

84. B.M. Add. MSS. 48,216.

85. *Full Report*, p. 52.

86. B.M. Add MSS. 48,216.

87. Old Bailey Sessions Papers, p. 268.

88. B.M. Add. MSS. 48,216; Storch, p. 139.

89. B.M. Add. MSS. 48,216; *Liverpool Mercury*, 15 May.

90. Old Bailey Sessions Papers, p. 268.

91. Ibid., pp. 270–71; St Neots Parish Registers; Bishop's Transcripts, Will of Edward Billett junior, 1791, Huntingdon Archives; Boyle's Court Guide, 1809.

92. P.R.O. Prob. 11/1485, 1486; Wilson, p. 39; Brooke, p. 481.

93. Old Bailey Sessions Papers, p. 271.

94. *European Magazine*, p. 377.

95. P.R.O. T/1243; *European Magazine*, p. 378.

96. *European Magazine*, p. 378.

97. Old Bailey Sessions Papers, p. 271.

98. P.R.O. 30/29/6/11.

99. *Freeman's Journal*, 18 May 1812; Hodgson, p. 85.

100. B.M. Add. MSS. 48,216.

101. Ibid.; *Freeman's Journal*, 18 May.

102. This and next two letters, *European Magazine*, pp. 378–9.

103. Hodgson, pp. 77–80.

104. Ibid.

105. P.R.O. T29/116/747.

106. P.R.O. T29/117/5215.

107. Hodgson, p. 83.

108. B.M. Add. MSS. 48,216.

109. *The Times*, 12 May; Old Bailey Sessions Papers, p. 272.

110. Hodgson, p. 82.

111. Old Bailey Sessions Papers, p. 266.

112. The report of Bellingham's conversation with Mary Stevens will be found in B.M. Add. MSS. 48,216.

113. Old Bailey Sessions Papers, p. 272; Hodgson, p. 86. Bellingham's laundry book is in B.M. Add. MSS. 48,216.

114. *Courier*, 14 May.

115. Details of the trial, other than those identified, may be found in Trial (1); *Morning Chronicle; Courier*.

116. Holland, Bk. II, p. 131.

117. *Courier*, 15 May; Old Bailey Sessions Papers, p. 270.

118. *European Magazine*, p. 369.

119. Brougham, vol. 2, p. 19.

120. The ensuing dialogue comes from Fraser, p. 2, and *Morning Chronicle*, 16 May.

121. *Liverpool Mercury*, 22 May.

122. *Morning Chronicle*, 16 May.

123. The speech of the Attorney-General which follows comes chiefly from Fraser and the *Morning Chronicle*.

124. *Authentic Account*, p. 43.

125. Old Bailey Sessions Papers, p. 267.

126. *Morning Chronicle*, 16 May.

127. Townsend, vol. 1, p. 318.

128. Bellingham's defence speech is from *Authentic Account*, pp. 24–37.

129. Townsend, vol. 1, p. 317.

130. Old Bailey Sessions Papers, 270–72.

131. Ibid., p. 272.

132. Chief Justice Mansfield's speech, Hodgson, pp. 87–9.

133. Hodgson, p. 90; *Morning Chronicle*, 16 May.

134. Fisher, pp. 9–10.

135. *European Magazine*, May 1812, vol. 61, p. 390.

136. *Freeman's Journal*, 28 May; *Notes and Queries*, 7 S. XI, p. 416, 23 May 1891.

137. *Morning Chronicle*, 19 May; Malmesbury, vol. 2, p. 282.

138. *Courier*, 18 May; Neild, p. 423.

139. *Courier*, 18 May.

140. Romilly, vol. 2, p. 257.

141. Holland, Bk. II, p. 130.

142. B.M. Add. MSS. 48,216.

143. *Morning Chronicle*, 13 and 16 May.

144. *Sun*, 16 May; *Courier*, 18 May.

145. *Morning Chronicle*, 19 May; *Public Ledger*, 19 May; *Sun*, 18 May.

146. H.M.C., Dropmore MSS, vol. 10, p. 255.

147. Trinity College Archives; Brooke, p. 483; Montagu, pp. 21, 48; *Gentleman's Magazine*, 1824, vol. 94, pt 1, p. 644.

148. Neild, p. 428, 423.

149. Wilson, pp. 2–25.

150. Bateman, vol. 1, p. 138.

151. H.M.C., Dropmore MSS, vol. 10, p. 251.

152. Buckingham (2), vol. 1, p. 299.

153. Hodgson, p. 93.

154. *Sun*, 18 May; *Liverpool Mercury*, 29 May; *Public Ledger*, 20 May.

155. *European Magazine*, pp. 454, 389. The letter was also widely published in the newspapers.

156. *National Adviser*, 19 May; *Public Ledger*, 19 May. Unattributed details that follow come from a variety of contemporary newspapers, including *National Adviser, Public Ledger, The Times, Morning Chronicle, Courier, Sun, Liverpool Mercury.*

157. *Morning Chronicle*, 19 May.

158. Montagu, p. 48.

159. Byron, vol. 1, p. 138.

160. *Political Register*, 23 May, vol. 21, No. 21, col. 669.

161. Cobbett, para. 133.

162. Ibid., para. 132.

163. *Morning Chronicle*, 21 May.

164. P.R.O. 30/29/6/11.

165. *Full Report*, p. 51.

166. *Political Register*, 30 May, vol. 21, No. 22, col. 674.

167. Knapp and Baldwin, vol. 4, pp. 82, 92.

168. Townsend, vol. 1, p. 318; Warren, vol. 2, p. 148.

169. *Morning Chronicle*, 10 June.

170. P.R.O. 30/29/6/11.

171. *Letters to John Drinkwater*, library transcript of letters in the possession of Major Drinkwater, Isle of Man [Prepared in Liverpool City Library 1960].

172. P.R.O. 30/29/6/11.

173. Ibid.

174. *Dublin Journal*, 2 June.

175. P.R.O. 30/29/6/11 and various journals.

176. P.R.O. 30/29/6/11.

177. Ibid.

178. *European Magazine*, p. 454.

179. All foregoing quotations in this chapter from P.R.O. 30/29/6/11.

180. Law List, 1812.

181. *Newcastle Journal*, 6 June.

182. *Notes and Queries*, 7 S. XI, 14 February, 1891, p. 121.

183. Colchester, vol. 2, p. 386.

184. MacNaghten, pp. 64, 66.

185. *Annual Register*, 1843, p. 361.

186. Prichard, p. 129.
187. MacNaghten, p. 45.
188. Raikes, vol. 4, p. 249.
189. *Liverpool Mercury*, 15 May; *Freeman's Journal*, Dublin, 28 May.
190. *European Magazine*, May 1812, vol. 61, p. 454.
191. *Perth Courier*, 28 May.
192. *Quarterly Review*, vol. 7–8, p. 349.
193. *Liverpool Mercury*, 28 May.
194. *European Magazine*, May 1812, vol. 61, p. 454; P.R.O. 30/29/6/11.
195. P.R.O. 30/29/6/11; Gore's Liverpool Directories.
196. B.M. Add. MSS. 49,188.
197. *Journals of the House of Commons*, vol. 67, p. 376.
198. *Edinburgh Review*, in the *Liverpool Mercury*, 25 September 1812.
199. *Monthly Magazine*, 1812, pt 1, p. 485.
200. Roberts, p. 167; Aspinall, vol. 1, p. 74; *Courier*, 15 May.
201. *Notes and Queries*, 7 S. 4, pp. 87, 217, 336–7, 493.

Bibliography

MANUSCRIPT SOURCES

British Museum Additional Manuscripts (BM Add. MSS): Perceval Papers
Crossle, F. C., 'Newry Jottings', MSS. 2202–2234, Dublin
Greater London Record Office (G.L.R.O.)
India Office Records (I.O.R.)
Parish Registers and Bishop's Transcripts
Public Record Office (P.R.O.): Granville Papers
Guildhall Records, Hull
Rate Books
Society of Friends, Records of births, marriages, burials
Williams, J. F., 'Being desired to write out the particulars of a remarkable dream . . .'

NEWSPAPERS AND PERIODICALS

Annual Register
Bell's Messenger
Courier
Daily Universal Register
Dublin Journal
Edinburgh Journal
Edinburgh Review
Edinburgh Weekly Chronicle
European Magazine, vol. 61, January–June 1812
Examiner
Freeman's Journal, Dublin
General Evening Post
Gentleman's Magazine
Hull Advertiser
Lady's Magazine
Liverpool Mercury
Moniteur Universel
Monthly Magazine
Moore's Almanack
Morning Chronicle
Morning Post
National Adviser
National Register
Newcastle Journal
Northampton Mercury

Notes and Queries   *Public Ledger*
Nottingham Journal   *Quarterly Review*
Observer   *Royal Kalendar*
Oracle   *St James's Chronicle*
Perth Courier   *Sun*
Political Register   *The Times*
Public Advertiser   *True Briton*

Selected Published Sources

Ackermann, R., *Microcosm of London*, 3 vols, London, 1808.

Aspinall, A. (ed.), *The Letters of King George IV, 1812–1830*, 3 vols, Cambridge University Press, London, 1938.

An Authentic Account of the Horrid Assassination of the Honourable Spencer Perceval, London, 1812.

Batchellor, John, *Thou Shalt Do No Murder! A Sermon*, London, 1812.

Bateman, Josiah, *The Life of the Right Reverend Daniel Wilson, D.D.*, 2 vols, John Murray, London, 1860.

Bath Archives: *Diaries and Letters of Sir George Jackson* – The Bath Archives, 1809–1816, ed. Lady Jackson, 2 vols, Richard Bentley, London, 1873.

Berry, Mary, *Journals and Correspondence of Miss Berry*, ed. Lady Theresa Lewis, 3 vols, Longmans Green, London, 1865.

Besant, Sir Walter, *London in the Eighteenth Century*, Adam & Charles Black, London, 1902.

——, *London in the Nineteenth Century*, Adam & Charles Black, London, 1909.

——, *Survey of London: North of the Thames*, Adam & Charles Black, London, 1911.

Bessborough: *Lady Bessborough and her family circle*, ed. by the Earl of Bessborough and A. Aspinall, John Murray, London, 1940.

Bleackley, H. W., *The Hangmen of England*, Chapman and Hall, London, 1929.

Brayley, E. W., and Britton, J., *The History of the Ancient Palace and late Houses of Parliament at Westminster*, London, 1836.

British Factory, *A Sketch drawn from the Records of the British Factory at St Petersburg*, London, 1824.

Brooke, Richard, *Liverpool during the last quarter of the eighteenth century*, Liverpool, 1853.

Brougham, *The Life and Times of Henry, Lord Brougham, by himself*, 3 vols, Harper Brothers, New York, 1871.

Buckingham, (1) Duke of, *Courts and Cabinets of George III*, 4 vols, Hurst & Blackett, London, 1853.
——, (2) *Court of England during the Regency*, 2 vols, Hurst & Blackett, London, 1856.
Bury, Lady Charlotte, *Diary of the Times of George IV*, 2 vols, Henry Colburn, London, 1838.
Butterworth, Joseph, *Complete Religious Liberty Vindicated . . . With remarks on the . . . correspondence between the Reverend Joseph Ivimey and Joseph Butterworth . . .*, by John Evans, London, 1813.
Byron, *A Self-Portrait*, ed. Peter Quennell, 2 vols, John Murray, London, 1950.
Callow, E., *Old London Taverns*, Downey & Co., London, 1899.
Calvert: *An Irish Beauty of the Regency: compiled from . . . the unpublished journals of the Hon. Mrs. Calvert, 1789–1822*, by Mrs Warrenne Blake, John Lane the Bodley Head, London, 1911.
Carr, John, *A Northern Summer*, Richard Phillips, London, 1805.
Chalmers, George, *An Appeal to the Generosity of the British Nation . . . on behalf of the afflicted Widow and unoffending Offspring of the unfortunate Mr Bellingham*, London, 1812.
Clarke, E. D., *Travels in various countries*, London, 1810.
Cobbett, William, *History of the Regency and Reign of George IV*, London, 1830.
Colchester, *The Diary and Correspondence of Charles Abbot, Lord Colchester*, 3 vols, John Murray, London, 1861.
Colquhoun, J. C., *William Wilberforce, his friends and his times*, Longmans Green, London, 1866.
Cotton, Sir Evan, *East Indiamen, The East India Company's Maritime Service*, ed. Sir Charles Fawcett, The Batchworth Press, London, 1949.
Coxe, William, *Travels in Russia*; in *A General Collection of the best and most interesting voyages and travels* by John Pinkerton, vol. 6, London, 1809.
Directories:
  London
  Boyle's Court Guide, 1798, 1800, 1804, 1807–9, 1812
  City of London, 1777
  Holden's, 1811
  Kent's, 1778–9, 1781–2, 1785–6, 1794, 1812
  London, 1778–9
  Lowndes, 1784, 1786
  New Complete Guide, 1783
  Post Office Annual, 1810, 1812
  Wakefield's Merchant's and Tradesman's General, 1790, 1794
  Liverpool
  Gore's, 1800–5, 1807, 1810–11, 1813, 1816, 1818, 1821, 1823, 1825, 1827, 1829, 1834.
Dixon, Hepworth, *The London Prisons*, Jackson and Walford, London, 1850.
Eldon, Lord, *The Public and Private Life of Lord Chancellor Eldon*, by Horace Twiss, 3 vols, John Murray, London, 1844.

Farington, Joseph, *The Farington Diary*, ed. James Grieg, 8 vols, Hutchinson, London, 1922–8.

Fisher, *National Portrait Gallery ... with memoirs by William Jerdan*, 5 vols, London, 1830–35.

Forbes, John, *An Account of the Trial of John Bellingham*, Brighton, 1812.

Fraser, *The Trial of John Bellingham*, London, 1812.

A Full Report of the Trial of John Bellingham, Hull, 1812.

A funeral discourse on the death of ... Right Honourable Spencer Perceval, London, 1812.

Gilbert, Linney, *Russia*, illustrated by A. G. Vickers.

Gordon, Charles, *The Old Bailey and Newgate*, T. Fisher Unwin, London, 1902.

Gorham, G. C., *History and Antiquities of Eynesbury and St Neots*, London, 1820.

Gower, Lord Granville Leveson (First Earl Granville): *Private Correspondence 1781–1821*, ed. Castalia Countess Granville, 2 vols, John Murray, London, 1916.

Graves, Algernon, *The Society of Artists of Great Britain 1760–1791. The Free Society of Artists 1761–1783*, George Bell & Sons, London, 1907.

Gray, Denis, *Spencer Perceval, The Evangelical Prime Minister*, Manchester University Press, Manchester, 1963.

Gray, Robert, D.D., *A Discourse, preached at Bishopwearmouth Church ... with reference to the assassination of the Right Honourable Spencer Perceval*, Sunderland, 1812.

Grellet: *Memoirs ... of Stephen Grellet*, ed. Benjamin Seebohm, 2 vols, Henry Longstreth, Philadelphia, 1864.

Griffiths, Arthur, *Chronicles of Newgate*, Chapman and Hall, London, 1896.

Hansard, T.C., *Parliamentary Debates*, Ser. 1, vol. 23, 5 May–30 July 1812.

Hassall, C., *Edward Marsh, Patron of the Arts*, Longmans, London, 1959.

Hastings, M., *Parliament House*, Architectural Press, London, 1950.

H.M.C.: Historical Manuscripts Commission, Dropmore MSS, vol. 10, 1927.

Hodgson, T., *A full and authentic report of the Trial of John Bellingham, Esq.*, London, 1812.

Holland, Lord, *Further Memoirs of the Whig Party*, ed. Lord Stavordale, John Murray, London, 1905.

House of Commons: *Biographical List of the House of Commons elected in October 1812*, Longman & Co., London, 1813.

Jackson, Sir George, *Diaries and Letters of Sir George Jackson*, ed. Lady Jackson, 2 vols, Richard Bentley, London, 1872.

Jerdan, William, *Autobiography*, 4 vols, Arthur Hall, Virtue & Co., London, 1852.

Jerningham: *The Jerningham Letters 1780–1843*, ed. Egerton Castle, 2 vols, Richard Bentley, London, 1896.

Journals of the House of Commons, The, vol. 67, 7 January – 30 July, 1812.

Jowett, Rev. Joseph, *A sermon ... The Vanity of Earthly Confidences*, Newark, 1812.

Knapp, Andrew, and Baldwin, William, *The Newgate Calendar*, 4 vols, London, 1824–6.

Laurence, J., *A History of Capital Punishment*, Sampson Low, Marston & Co., London, 1932.

Law List, various years.

Lincoln's Inn, *The Records of the Honourable Society of Lincoln's Inn*: The Black Books, vol. 4, 1902.

Liverpool Trade List, 26 July, 1798 – 24 December 1799.

Lloyd's List, 1803.

Lovat-Fraser, J. A., 'The Trial of Bellingham', *Juridical Review*, 1917, pp. 62–8.

MacNaghten, Daniel: *Report of the Trial* . . . , by R. M. Bousfield and R. Merrett, London, 1843.

Malmesbury, 1st Earl, *Letters* . . . *1745–1820*, 2 vols, Richard Bentley, London, 1870.

May, L. M., *Charlton* . . . , London, 1908.

Mayhew, H. and Binny, J., *The Criminal Prisons of London*, London, 1862.

Montagu, Basil, *An Inquiry into the Aspersions upon the late Ordinary of Newgate*, London, 1815.

Neild, James, *State of the Prisons in England, Scotland and Wales*, London, 1812.

Northampton: *Records of the Borough of Northampton*, 2 vols, ed. C. A. Markham and Rev. J. C. Cox, Northampton, 1898.

Old Bailey Sessions Papers, 1811–12.

Parker, W. H., *An Historical Geography of Russia*, University of London Press, London, 1968.

Peck, Robert, *Trial of John Bellingham*, Hull, 1812.

Prichard, James Cowles, M.D., *On the different forms of insanity* . . . , London, 1842.

Pringle, P., *The Thief-Takers*, Museum Press, London, 1958.

Raikes, T., *Journal*, 4 vols, Longman, London, 1857.

Rayner, J. L. (ed.) and Crook, G. T. (ed.), *Complete Newgate Calendar*, Navarre Society, London, 1925–6.

Redgrave, R. and S., *A Century of Painters of the English School*, 2 vols, Smith, Elder & Co., London, 1866.

Roberts, W. (A Barrister), *The Portraiture of a Christian Gentleman*, London, 1829.

Romilly, Sir Samuel, *Memoirs*, ed. by his sons, 2 vols, John Murray, London, 1841.

Scenes in Russia (anon.), London, 1814.

Shelley, H. C., *Inns and Taverns of Old London*, Sir Isaac Pitman, London, 1909.

Sibthorp, Rev. R. W., *Substance of a Sermon* . . . *following the interment of Joseph Butterworth*, 1826.

Smith, John G., *Charlton. A Compilation of the Parish and its People* . . . 1970.

Smith, John T., *A Book for a Rainy Day*, Methuen, London, 1905.

Smith, John T., *Antiquities of Westminster*, London, 1809.

Smith, W., *A List of Bankrupts* . . . *January 1786 – June 1806*, London, 1806.

Stephen, James F., *A Digest of the Law of Evidence*, Macmillan, London, 1876.

Storch, Henry, *Picture of Petersburg*, Longman, London, 1801.

Townsend, W. C., *Modern State Trials*, 2 vols, Longman, London, 1850.

Trial (1): *Trial of John Bellingham* . . . London, 1812 (J. Morton).

Trial (2): *Trial of J. Bellingham* . . . London, 1812 (for the Booksellers).

University of Dublin, A *Catalogue of Graduates* . . . *to July 1866*, Dublin, 1869.

Van Mildert, W., *A sermon preached before the Honourable Society of Lincoln's Inn* . . . *1812 to 1819*, 2 vols, Oxford, 1831.

Victoria History of the Counties of England: Huntingdonshire.

Walpole, Sir Spencer, *Life of the Right Honourable Spencer Perceval*, 2 vols, London, 1874.

Ward, John, *Letters to Ivy from the 1st Earl of Dudley*, ed. S. H. Romilly, Longmans Green, London, 1905.

Ward, Robert Plumer, *Memoirs*, ed. Hon. Edmund Phipps, 2 vols, John Murray, London, 1850.

Warren, Samuel, *Miscellanie, Critical, Imaginative and Juridical*, 2 vols, William Blackwood, Edinburgh and London, 1855.

Watson, Rev. R., *A Sermon on the Death of Joseph Butterworth, Esq.*, London, 1826.

Whitley, T. W., *The Parliamentary Representation of the City of Coventry*, Curtis and Beamish, Coventry, 1892–4.

Whitefoord, Caleb: *The Whitefoord Papers*, ed. W. A. S. Hewins, Clarendon Press, Oxford, 1898.

Williams' Law and Practice in Bankruptcy, 17th ed., London, 1958.

Williams, C. V., *Life and Administration of the Right Honourable Spencer Perceval*, London, 1812.

Williams, Orlo Cyprian, *The Topography of the Old House of Commons*, London, 1953.

Wilson, Rev. Daniel, *Substance of a conversation with John Bellingham*, London, 1812.

Zacek, Judith C., *Canadian Slavic Studies*, I, no. 2 (summer, 1967), pp. 196–211: 'A case study in Russian philanthropy'.

Index